# 2013 SUPPLEMENT TO

# INTELLECTUAL PROPERTY

## CASES AND MATERIALS

**Fourth Edition**

■ ■ ■

By

**Margreth Barrett**
*Professor of Law Emeritus*
*University of California*
*Hastings College of Law*

AMERICAN CASEBOOK SERIES®

WEST®

Mat #41355599

610 Opperman Drive
St. Paul, MN 55123
1-800-313-9378



Printed in the United States of America

**ISBN:** 978–0–314–28622–2

# Preface

This Supplement updates my case book, Intellectual Property Cases and Materials (4th ed., Thomson/West Publishers, 2011) through the summer of 2013. Both the courts and Congress have been busy since 2011. Perhaps most importantly, Congress enacted the Leahy-Smith America Invents Act, Pub. L. No. 112-29, 125 Stat. 284 (2011), which has been hailed as the most comprehensive U.S. patent reform since the Patent Act of 1952. The product of six years of concentrated Congressional effort, the America Invents Act moves the United States from its long-cherished "first-to-invent" system to a "first-inventor-to-file" system, thus harmonizing United States patent protection with world patent norms. Among other things, the Act significantly extends prior user rights, and provides a range of reworked and new administrative procedures for reviewing and challenging patent applications and issued patents in the Patent and Trademark Office. These new procedures are aimed at improving patent quality and reducing litigation costs.

Some of the Act's provisions became effective on September 16, 2011, while many of the more complex provisions only became effective September 16, 2012, or March 16, 2013. Most of the new provisions only apply prospectively, requiring courts and the Patent Office to continue applying pre-America Invents Act laws to pre-existing applications and patents for years to come.

The Supreme Court has also handed down a number of important decisions in both the Patent and the Copyright area. This Supplement either reproduces or discusses: (1) *Mayo Collaborative Services v. Prometheus Laboratories, Inc.* (patentable subject matter—medical diagnostic methods); (2) *Association for Molecular Pathology v. Myriad Genetics, Inc.* (patentable subject matter—gene patents); (3) *Bowman v. Monsanto Co.* (patent doctrine of first sale in the case of self-replicating inventions); (4) *Global-Tech Appliances, Inc. v. SEB S.A.* (actionable knowledge for purposes of patent infringement inducement claims); (5) *Microsoft Corp. v. i4i Partnership,* (standard of proof needed to prove patent invalidity); (5) *Kirtsaeng v. John Wiley & Sons, Inc.* (the reach of copyright law's doctrine of exhaustion to parallel Imports manufactured abroad); and *Golan v. Holder* (upholding the constitutionality of foreign copyright restoration provisions).

The Supplement also includes or discusses a number of important decisions from the U.S. Circuit Courts of Appeal, including: (1) *CyberSource Corp v. Retail Decisions, Inc.* (software-related inventions as patentable subject matter); (2) *CLS Bank International v. Alice Corp.* (*en banc* Federal Circuit struggles with software inventions as patentable subject matter); (3) *Akamai Technologies, Inc. v. Limelight Networks, Inc.* (*en banc* Federal Circuit addresses "direct infringement" for purposes of holding a third party liable for inducement); (4) *Therasense, Inc. v. Becton, Dickenson & Co.* (*en banc* Federal Circuit addresses proof necessary to demonstrate inequitable conduct); (5) *Network Automation, Inc. v. Advanced Systems Concepts, Inc.* (Ninth Circuit evaluates the likelihood of consumer confusion in contextual advertising cases); and *Robert Bosch LLC v. Pylon Manufacturing Corp.* (Federal Circuit evaluates proof of irreparable harm in injunction analysis).

This Supplement follows the existing structure of the case book, and provides changes and additions to the text by page number, as they fit into the existing case book discussion. As in the case book, I have deleted citations and footnotes from reproduced materials without express indication. Deleted text is expressly indicated with three asterisks.

Margreth Barrett
San Francisco
July, 2013

# Table of Contents

**CHAPTER FOUR: COPYRIGHT**



**CHAPTER FIVE: TRADEMARKS AND OTHER INDICATIONS OF ORIGIN**

# Chapter 3

# PATENTS

## 1. UTILITY PATENTS

## A. INTRODUCTION

*Pages 123-24, Note 1, second paragraph:*

The America Invents Act (hereafter "AIA") renames the Board of Patent Appeals and Interferences and expands its jurisdiction. It is to be called the Patent Trial and Appeal Board. Pub. L. No. 112-29 § 7, 125 Stat. 313 (2011).

In addition, the new Act moves the venue for district court review of Board decisions from the U.S. District Court for the District of Columbia to the U.S. District Court for the Eastern District of Virginia. This change is effective on September 16, 2011, and applies to all civil actions commenced on or after that date. Pub. L. No. 112-29, 125 Stat. 316 (2011). The change probably reflects the fact that the Patent and Trademark Office has moved from the District of Columbia to Alexandria, Virginia.

*Page 131, Note 2, last two paragraphs:*

America Invents Act §19 (b) amends 28 U.S.C. § 1295(a)(1) to provide that the United States Court of Appeals for the Federal Circuit has jurisdiction over appeals in "any civil action arising under, or in any civil action in which a party has asserted a compulsory counterclaim arising under, any Act of Congress relating to patents * * *" This amendment is effective for any civil action commenced on or after September 16, 2011. It should effectively neutralize the *Holms Group v. Vornado Air Circulation* decision and consolidate all appellate review of patent issues in the Federal Circuit. Pub. L. No. 112-29 § 19, 125 Stat. 331 (2011).

# B. THE SUBJECT MATTER OF UTILITY PATENTS

*Page 140, Note 2, at the end of the first full paragraph, add the following:*

America Invents Act § 33(a) provides: "Notwithstanding any other provision of law, no patent may issue on a claim directed to or encompassing a human organism." This provision applies to any application for patent that was pending on, or filed on or after September 16, 2011. Pub. L. No. 112-29 § 33, 125 Stat. 340 (2011). A similar prohibition has been enacted in the past as part of the Patent Office's annual appropriations legislation. When does a claim "encompass" a human organism? Does this prohibition extend to biotechnological methods of treating human illness?

*Page 141, add the following new Note 3, and renumber existing Note 3 Note 4:*

*3. Patents for isolated DNA segments: The Supreme Court's decision in Assn. for Molecular Pathology v. Myriad Genetics, Inc.* Myriad Genetics discovered the precise location and sequence of two human genes (BRCA1 and BRCA2), mutations of which can dramatically increase an individual's risk of breast and ovarian cancer. This discovery enabled Myriad to develop medical tests for detecting mutations in those genes in a particular patient (by extracting DNA from the patient's cells and isolating the specific gene segments) to assess the patient's risk of cancer. Myriad obtained a number of patents based upon its discovery, which included composition claims for (1) the isolated gene DNA segments and (2) synthetically created strands of nucleotides known as composite DNA (cDNA), which reproduce the DNA segment's exons (which code for amino acids) but not the DNA segment's introns (which do not). If valid, the patents would give Myriad the exclusive right to isolate an individual's BRCA1 and BRCA2 gene, and would give Myriad the exclusive right to synthetically create BRCA cDNA. The question before the Supreme Court was whether a naturally occurring segment of DNA is patent eligible by virtue of its isolation from the rest of the human genome. In addition, the Court considered whether synthetically created DNA (cDNA) (which contains the same protein-coding information found in a segment of natural DNA but omits portions within the DNA segment that do not code for proteins) is patent eligible subject matter.

The Supreme Court began its analysis by noting the court-made exception to patentable subject matter for "laws of nature, natural phenomena, and abstract ideas," explaining that these things are "the basic tools of scientific and technological work." Patenting them would likely inhibit future innovation, rather than promote it. The Court then undertook to determine whether the isolated DNA claims merely sought to patent natural phenomena or "laws of nature," and thus failed to state patentable subject matter. It found that they did indeed claim unpatentable subject matter:

> It is undisputed that Myriad did not create or alter any of the genetic information encoded in the BRCA1 and BRCA2 genes. The location and order of the nucleotides existed in nature before Myriad found them. Nor did Myriad create or alter the genetic structure of DNA. Instead, Myriad's principal contribution was uncovering the precise location and genetic sequence of the BRCA1 and BRCA2 genes within chromosomes 17 and 13. The question is whether this renders the genes patentable.
>
> Myriad recognizes that our decision in *Chakrabarty* is central to this inquiry. In *Chakrabarty,* scientists added four plasmids to a bacterium, which enabled it to break down

various components of crude oil. The Court held that the modified bacterium was patentable. It explained that the patent claim was "not to a hitherto unknown natural phenomenon, but to a nonnaturally occurring manufacture or composition of matter—a product of human ingenuity 'having a distinctive name, character [and] use.'" The *Chakrabarty* bacterium was new "with markedly different characteristics from any found in nature," due to the additional plasmids and resultant "capacity for degrading oil." In this case, by contrast, Myriad did not create anything. To be sure, it found an important and useful gene, but separating that gene from its surrounding genetic material is not an act of invention.

Groundbreaking, innovative, or even brilliant discovery does not by itself satisfy the § 101 inquiry. In *Funk Brothers Seed Co. v. Kalo Inoculant Co.,* 333 U.S. 127, (1948), this Court considered a composition patent that claimed a mixture of naturally occurring strains of bacteria that helped leguminous plants take nitrogen from the air and fix it in the soil. The ability of the bacteria to fix nitrogen was well known, and farmers commonly "inoculated" their crops with them to improve soil nitrogen levels. But farmers could not use the same inoculant for all crops, both because plants use different bacteria and because certain bacteria inhibit each other. Upon learning that several nitrogen-fixing bacteria did not inhibit each other, however, the patent applicant combined them into a single inoculant and obtained a patent. The Court held that the composition was not patent eligible because the patent holder did not alter the bacteria in any way. * * * His patent claim thus fell squarely within the law of nature exception. So do Myriad's. Myriad found the location of the BRCA1 and BRCA2 genes, but that discovery, by itself, does not render the BRCA genes "new ... composition[s] of matter," § 101, that are patent eligible.

* * *

Nor are Myriad's claims saved by the fact that isolating DNA from the human genome severs chemical bonds and thereby creates a nonnaturally occurring molecule. Myriad's

> claims are simply not expressed in terms of chemical composition, nor do they rely in any way on the chemical changes that result from the isolation of a particular section of DNA. Instead, the claims understandably focus on the genetic information encoded in the BRCA1 and BRCA2 genes. If the patents depended upon the creation of a unique molecule, then a would-be infringer could arguably avoid at least Myriad's patent claims on entire genes (such as claims 1 and 2 of the '282 patent) by isolating a DNA sequence that included both the BRCA1 or BRCA2 gene and one additional nucleotide pair. Such a molecule would not be chemically identical to the molecule "invented" by Myriad. But Myriad obviously would resist that outcome because its claim is concerned primarily with the information contained in the genetic *sequence,* not with the specific chemical composition of a particular molecule.

However, the Supreme Court found that the cDNA claims stated patentable subject matter:

> cDNA does not present the same obstacles to patentability as naturally occurring, isolated DNA segments. As already explained, creation of a cDNA sequence from mRNA results in an exons-only molecule that is not naturally occurring. Petitioners concede that cDNA differs from natural DNA in that "the non-coding regions have been removed." They nevertheless argue that cDNA is not patent eligible because "[t]he nucleotide sequence of cDNA is dictated by nature, not by the lab technician." That may be so, but the lab technician unquestionably creates something new when cDNA is made. cDNA retains the naturally occurring exons of DNA, but it is distinct from the DNA from which it was derived. As a result, cDNA is not a "product of nature" and is patent eligible under § 101, except insofar as very short series of DNA may have no intervening introns to remove when creating cDNA. In that situation, a short strand of cDNA may be indistinguishable from natural DNA.

Having reached this "compromise" position, the Court cautioned against reading its decision too broadly:

> It is important to note what is *not* implicated by this decision. First, there are no method claims before this Court. Had Myriad created an innovative method of manipulating genes while searching for the BRCA1 and BRCA2 genes, it could possibly have sought a method patent. But the processes used by Myriad to isolate DNA were well understood by geneticists at the time of Myriad's patents "were well understood, widely used, and fairly uniform insofar as any scientist engaged in the search for a gene would likely have utilized a similar approach," and are not at issue in this case.
>
> Similarly, this case does not involve patents on new *applications* of knowledge about the BRCA1 and BRCA2 genes. Judge Bryson aptly noted that, "[a]s the first party with knowledge of the [BRCA1 and BRCA2] sequences, Myriad was in an excellent position to claim applications of that knowledge. Many of its unchallenged claims are limited to such applications."
>
> Nor do we consider the patentability of DNA in which the order of the naturally occurring nucleotides has been altered. Scientific alteration of the genetic code presents a different inquiry, and we express no opinion about the application of § 101 to such endeavors. We merely hold that genes and the information they encode are not patent eligible under § 101 simply because they have been isolated from the surrounding genetic material.

Association for Molecular Pathology v. Myriad Genetics, Inc., __ U.S. __, __ S.Ct. __, 2013 W.L. 2630162 (2013). Did the court provide sufficient guidance for determining whether a claimed composition of matter is "naturally occurring?" Today companies manufacture proteins and antibodies that closely mimic those naturally produced by the body. How much must they differ from from the naturally occurring proteins and antibodies in order to constitute patentable subject matter? Assume that a scientist takes a chemical that exists in nature in combination with other substances and purifies it—will purification (so that the chemical exists by itself) be sufficient to render the chemical composition patentable? The *Myriad* Court's analysis invalidated claims directed to DNA sequences in thousands of patents. Most of these patents were granted in the mid-and late 1990's and thus would have expired within the next few years. Given that cDNA claims were upheld, it is difficult to determine how strongly the decision will affect biotechnology industries. The *Myriad* Court stresses that its decision does not address the validity of patents for methods of applying discoveries such as Myriad's. After reading the *Mayo* decision, *infra,* consider the likely validity of Myriad's method patents claiming use of the BRCA gene mutations to assess a patient's risk of cancer.

*Pages 154-161, directly following the Bilski decision--Replace the Notes and Questions and Problem with the following:*

## Mayo Collaborative Services v. Prometheus Laboratories, Inc.

United States Supreme Court, 2012.
566 U.S. __, 132 S.Ct. 1289, 18 L.Ed.2d 321.

Justice BREYER delivered the opinion of the Court.

Section 101 of the Patent Act defines patentable subject matter. It says:

> "Whoever invents or discovers any new and useful process, machine, manufacture, or composition of matter, or any new and useful improvement thereof, may obtain a patent therefor, subject to the conditions and requirements of this title." 35 U.S.C. § 101.

The Court has long held that this provision contains an important implicit exception. "[L]aws of nature, natural phenomena, and abstract ideas" are not patentable. * * * [M]onopolization of those tools through the grant of a patent might tend to impede innovation more than it would tend to promote it.

The Court has recognized, however, that too broad an interpretation of this exclusionary principle could eviscerate patent law. For all inventions at some level embody, use, reflect, rest upon, or apply laws of nature, natural phenomena, or abstract ideas. Thus, in [*Diamond v. Diehr,* 450 US. 175, 187 (1980)], the Court pointed out that " 'a process is not unpatentable simply because it contains a law of nature or a mathematical algorithm.'" It added that "an *application* of a law of nature or mathematical formula to a known structure or process may well be deserving of patent protection." * * *

Still, as the Court has also made clear, to transform an unpatentable law of nature into a patent-eligible *application* of such a law, one must do more than simply state the law of nature while adding the words "apply it."

The case before us lies at the intersection of these basic principles. It concerns patent claims covering processes that help doctors who use thiopurine drugs to treat patients with autoimmune diseases determine whether a given dosage level is too low or too high. The claims purport to apply natural laws describing the relationships between the concentration in the blood of certain thiopurine metabolites and the likelihood that the drug dosage will be ineffective or induce harmful side-effects. We must determine whether the claimed processes have transformed these unpatentable natural laws into patent-eligible applications of those laws. We conclude that they have not done so and that therefore the processes are not patentable.

Our conclusion rests upon an examination of the particular claims before us in light of the Court's precedents. Those cases warn us against interpreting patent statutes in ways that make patent eligibility "depend simply on the draftsman's art" without reference to the "principles underlying the prohibition against patents for [natural laws]." [*Parker v. Flook,* 437 U.S. 584, 593 (1978)]. They warn us against upholding patents that claim processes that too broadly preempt the use of a natural law. And they insist that a process that focuses upon the use of a natural law also contain other elements or a combination of elements, sometimes referred to as an "inventive concept," sufficient to ensure that the patent in practice amounts to significantly more than a patent upon the natural law itself. * * *

We find that the process claims at issue here do not satisfy these conditions. In particular, the steps in the claimed processes (apart from the natural laws themselves) involve well-understood, routine, conventional activity previously engaged in by researchers in the field. At the same time, upholding the patents would risk disproportionately tying up the use of the underlying natural laws, inhibiting their use in the making of further discoveries.

I

A

The patents before us concern the use of thiopurine drugs in the treatment of autoimmune diseases, such as Crohn's disease and ulcerative colitis. When a patient ingests a thiopurine compound, his body metabolizes the drug, causing metabolites to form in his bloodstream. Because the way in which people metabolize thiopurine compounds varies, the same dose of a thiopurine drug affects different people differently, and it has been difficult for doctors to determine whether for a particular patient a given dose is too high, risking harmful side effects, or too low, and so likely ineffective.

At the time the discoveries embodied in the patents were made, scientists already understood that the levels in a patient's blood of certain metabolites, including, in particular, 6–thioguanine and its nucleotides (6–TG) and 6–methyl–mercaptopurine (6–MMP), were correlated with the likelihood that a particular dosage of a thiopurine drug could cause harm or prove ineffective. * * * But those in the field did not know the precise correlations between metabolite levels and likely harm or ineffectiveness. The patent claims at issue here set forth processes embodying researchers' findings that identified these correlations with some precision.

More specifically, the patents—U.S. Patent No. 6,355,623 ('623 patent) and U.S. Patent No. 6,680,302 ('302 patent)—embody findings that concentrations in a patient's blood of 6–TG or of 6–MMP metabolite beyond a certain level (400 and 7000 picomoles per $8x10^8$ red blood cells, respectively) indicate that the dosage is likely too high for the patient, while concentrations in the blood of 6–TG metabolite lower than a certain level (about 230 picomoles per $8x10^8$ red blood cells) indicate that the dosage is likely too low to be effective.

The patent claims seek to embody this research in a set of processes. Like the Federal Circuit we take as typical claim 1 of the '623 Patent, which describes one of the claimed processes as follows:

> "A method of optimizing therapeutic efficacy for treatment of an immune-mediated gastrointestinal disorder, comprising:
> "(a) administering a drug providing 6–thioguanine to a subject having said immune-mediated gastrointestinal disorder; and
> "(b) determining the level of 6–thioguanine in said subject having said immune-mediated gastrointestinal disorder,
> "wherein the level of 6–thioguanine less than about 230 pmol per $8x10^8$ red blood cells indicates a need to increase the amount of said drug subsequently administered to said subject and
> "wherein the level of 6–thioguanine greater than about 400 pmol per $8x10^8$ red blood cells indicates a need to decrease the amount of said drug subsequently administered to said subject." '623 patent, col.20, ll.10–20, 2 App. 16.
> * * *

B

* * *

[The District Court] granted summary judgment in Mayo's favor. The court reasoned that the patents effectively claim natural laws or natural phenomena—namely the correlations between thiopurine metabolite levels and the toxicity and efficacy of thiopurine drug dosages—and so are not patentable.

On appeal, the Federal Circuit reversed. It pointed out that in addition to these natural correlations, the claimed processes specify the steps of (1) "administering a [thiopurine] drug" to a patient and (2) "determining the [resulting metabolite] level." These steps, it explained, involve the transformation of the human body or of blood taken from the body. Thus, the patents satisfied the Circuit's "machine or transformation test," which the court thought sufficient to "confine the patent monopoly within rather definite bounds," thereby bringing the claims into compliance with § 101. 581 F.3d 1336, 1345, 1346–1347 (2009).

* * *

II

Prometheus' patents set forth laws of nature—namely, relationships between concentrations of certain metabolites in the blood and the likelihood that a dosage of a thiopurine drug will prove ineffective or cause harm. Claim 1, for example, states that *if* the levels of 6–TG in the blood (of a patient who has taken a dose of a thiopurine drug) exceed about 400 pmol per $8x10^{8}$ red blood cells, *then* the administered dose is likely to produce toxic side effects. While it takes a human action (the administration of a thiopurine drug) to trigger a manifestation of this relation in a particular person, the relation itself exists in principle apart from any human action. The relation is a consequence of the ways in which thiopurine compounds are metabolized by the body—entirely natural processes. And so a patent that simply describes that relation sets forth a natural law.

The question before us is whether the claims do significantly more than simply describe these natural relations. To put the matter more precisely, do the patent claims add *enough* to their statements of the correlations to allow the processes they describe to qualify as patent-eligible processes that *apply* natural laws? We believe that the answer to this question is no.

A

If a law of nature is not patentable, then neither is a process reciting a law of nature, unless that process has additional features that provide practical assurance that the process is more than a drafting effort designed to monopolize the law of nature itself. A patent, for example, could not simply recite a law of nature and then add the instruction "apply the law." * * *

What else is there in the claims before us? The process that each claim recites tells doctors interested in the subject about the correlations that the researchers discovered. In doing so, it recites an "administering" step, a "determining" step, and a "wherein" step. These additional steps are not themselves natural laws but neither are they sufficient to transform the nature of the claim.

First, the "administering" step simply refers to the relevant audience, namely doctors who treat patients with certain diseases with thiopurine drugs. That audience is a pre-existing audience; doctors used thiopurine drugs to treat patients suffering from autoimmune disorders long before anyone asserted these claims. In any event, the "prohibition against patenting abstract ideas 'cannot be circumvented by attempting to limit the use of the formula to a particular technological environment.'" [*Bilski v. Kappos,* 561 U.S. __ (2010) (slip op., at 14)].

Second, the "wherein" clauses simply tell a doctor about the relevant natural laws, at most adding a suggestion that he should take those laws into account when treating his patient. That is to say, these clauses tell the relevant audience about the laws while trusting them to use those laws appropriately where they are relevant to their decisionmaking * * * .

Third, the "determining" step tells the doctor to determine the level of the relevant metabolites in the blood, through whatever process the doctor or the laboratory wishes to use. As the patents state, methods for determining metabolite levels were well known in the art. Indeed, scientists routinely measured metabolites as part of their investigations into the relationships between metabolite levels and efficacy and toxicity of thiopurine compounds. Thus, this step tells doctors to engage in well-understood, routine, conventional activity previously engaged in by scientists who work in the field. Purely "conventional or obvious" "[pre]-solution activity" is normally not sufficient to transform an unpatentable law of nature into a patent-eligible application of such a law. *Flook,* 437 U.S., at 590 * * *.

Fourth, to consider the three steps as an ordered combination adds nothing to the laws of nature that is not already present when the steps are considered separately. * * * Anyone who wants to make use of these laws must first administer a thiopurine drug and measure the resulting metabolite concentrations, and so the combination amounts to nothing significantly more than an instruction to doctors to apply the applicable laws when treating their patients.

The upshot is that the three steps simply tell doctors to gather data from which they may draw an inference in light of the correlations. To put the matter more succinctly, the claims inform a relevant audience about certain laws of nature; any additional steps consist of well-understood, routine, conventional activity already engaged in by the scientific community; and those steps, when viewed as a whole, add nothing significant beyond the sum of their parts taken separately. For these reasons we believe that the steps are not sufficient to transform unpatentable natural correlations into patentable applications of those regularities.

B

1

A more detailed consideration of the controlling precedents reinforces our conclusion. The cases most directly on point are *Diehr* and *Flook,* two cases in which the Court reached opposite conclusions about the patent eligibility of processes that embodied the equivalent of natural laws. The *Diehr* process (held patent eligible) set forth a method for molding raw, uncured rubber into various cured, molded products. The process used a known mathematical equation, the Arrhenius equation, to determine when (depending upon the temperature inside the mold, the time the rubber had been in the mold, and the thickness of the rubber) to open the press. It consisted in effect of the steps of: (1) continuously monitoring the temperature on the inside of the mold, (2) feeding the resulting numbers into a computer, which would use the Arrhenius equation to continuously recalculate the mold-opening time, and (3) configuring the computer so that at the appropriate moment it would signal "a device" to open the press. *Diehr,* 450 U.S., at 177–179.

The Court pointed out that the basic mathematical equation, like a law of nature, was not patentable. But it found the overall process patent eligible because of the way the additional steps of the process integrated the equation into the process as a whole. Those steps included "installing rubber in a press, closing the mold, constantly determining the temperature of the mold, constantly recalculating the appropriate cure time through the use of the formula and a digital computer, and automatically opening the press at the proper time." *Id.,* at 187. It nowhere suggested that all these steps, or at least the combination of those steps, were in context obvious, already in use, or purely conventional. And so the patentees did not "seek to pre-empt the use of [the] equation," but sought "only to foreclose from others the use of that equation in conjunction with all of the other steps in their claimed process." *Ibid.* These other steps apparently added to the formula something that in terms of patent law's objectives had significance—they transformed the process into an inventive application of the formula.

The process in *Flook* (held not patentable) provided a method for adjusting "alarm limits" in the catalytic conversion of hydrocarbons. Certain operating conditions (such as temperature, pressure, and flow rates), which are continuously monitored during the conversion process, signal inefficiency or danger when they exceed certain "alarm limits." The claimed process amounted to an improved system for updating those alarm limits through the steps of: (1) measuring the current level of the variable, *e.g.,* the temperature; (2) using an apparently novel mathematical algorithm to calculate the current alarm limits; and (3) adjusting the system to reflect the new alarm-limit values. 437 U.S., at 585–587.

The Court, as in *Diehr,* pointed out that the basic mathematical equation, like a law of nature, was not patentable. But it characterized the claimed process as doing nothing other than "provid[ing] a[n unpatentable] formula for computing an updated alarm limit." *Flook, supra,* at 586. Unlike the process in *Diehr,* it did not "explain how the variables used in the formula were to be selected, nor did the [claim] contain any disclosure relating to chemical processes at work or the means of setting off an alarm or adjusting the alarm limit." *Diehr, supra,* at 192, n. 14; see also *Flook,* 437 U.S., at 586. And so the other steps in the process did not limit the claim to a particular application. Moreover, "[t]he chemical processes involved in catalytic conversion of hydrocarbons[,] ... the practice of monitoring the chemical process variables, the use of alarm limits to trigger alarms, the notion that alarm limit values must be recomputed and readjusted, and the use of computers for 'automatic monitoring-alarming' " were all "well known," to the point where, putting the formula to the side, there was no "inventive concept" in the claimed application of the formula. *Id.,* at 594. "[P]ost-solution activity" that is purely "conventional or obvious," the Court wrote, "can[not] transform an unpatentable principle into a patentable process." *Id.,* at 589, 590.

The claim before us presents a case for patentability that is weaker than the (patent-eligible) claim in *Diehr* and no stronger than the (unpatentable) claim in *Flook.* Beyond picking out the relevant audience, namely those who administer doses of thiopurine drugs, the claim simply tells doctors to: (1) measure (somehow) the current level of the relevant metabolite, (2) use particular (unpatentable) laws of nature (which the claim sets forth) to calculate the current toxicity/inefficacy limits, and (3) reconsider the drug dosage in light of the law. These instructions add nothing specific to the laws of nature other than what is well-understood, routine, conventional activity, previously engaged in by those in the field. And since they are steps that must be taken in order to apply the laws in question, the effect is simply to tell doctors to apply the law somehow when treating their patients. The process in *Diehr* was not so characterized; that in *Flook* was characterized in roughly this way.

* * *

### *Notes and Questions*

1. *Laws of nature, natural phenomena and abstract ideas.* As the *Bilski* and *Mayo* opinions indicate, laws of nature, natural phenomena and abstract ideas are not patentable. Only *specific applications* of laws of nature, natural phenomena and abstract ideas can be patented. Thus, while Sir Isaac Newton could not obtain a patent for the law of gravity (which is a law of nature, natural phenomenon or abstract idea), one could obtain a patent for a new machine or process that applies or incorporates the law of gravity in its operation.

What is the justification for the rule that laws of nature, natural phenomena and abstract ideas are not themselves patentable? Why is a "field of use" restriction insufficient to avoid a finding that a claim states an abstract idea? Should it matter whether the law of nature or abstract idea at issue is narrow and specific or broad and general? For example, should the Supreme Court in *Mayo* have taken into account the narrowness of the law of nature at issue in that case? Arguably a patent on a narrow law of nature (such as the correlation between thiopurine metabolite levels and the toxicity and efficacy of thiopurine drug dosages) will not inhibit future research as seriously as would a patent on a broader law of nature, such as Einstein's law of relativity.

Is there a principled way to determine whether elements encompassed in claim language merely constitute "insignificant post-solution activity" or "well-understood, routine, conventional activity previously engaged in by those in the field"? Is the *Mayo* Court's distinction of the claims in *Diamond v. Diehr* from the claims in *Parker v. Flook* and *Mayo* convincing?

In light of the *Bilski* opinion, how would you define an "abstract idea"? Given the courts' difficulties in defining the limits of patentable subject matter, would it be preferable to abandon attempts to determine whether a claimed invention is merely an abstract idea, law of nature or natural phenomenon, and simply rely on the other requirements of patent eligibility (novelty, non-obviousness, disclosure) to eliminate inappropriate claims?

Did the *Mayo* court reach the right decision? What is the likely impact of the *Mayo* decision on investment in medical research—particularly in the area of diagnostic research?

2. *The machine-or-transformation standard.* How does the machine-or-transformation test (inquiring whether a claimed process is tied to a particular machine or apparatus or transforms a particular article into a different state or thing) ensure that a claimed process is more than an abstract idea? In *Bilski*, how did the majority determine that the claimed risk-hedging process merely constituted an abstract idea? Did it rely on the machine-or-transformation inquiry, or some other standard? If the latter, what was the standard? How would the machine-or-transformation standard apply in the *Mayo* case?

3. *Business methods as patentable "processes."* In State Street Bank & Trust Co. v. Signature Financial Group, Inc., 149 F.3d 1368 (Fed. Cir. 1998), *cert. denied*, 525 U.S. 1093 (1999), the patent applicant claimed a data processing system to implement a particular type of mutual fund investment structure in which two or more mutual funds pool their investment funds into a single portfolio, to consolidate administration costs and gain various tax advantages. The system enabled the investment structure administrator, among other things, to monitor and record financial information; allocate expenses, gains and losses on a daily basis among the participating mutual funds; and determine the value of each participating mutual fund's investment on any given day so that the value of publicly traded shares in the mutual fund could then be calculated. The claims for the system included elements of computer hardware. The Court of Appeals for the Federal Circuit found that the claims stated statutory subject matter—a machine.

The Federal Circuit rejected arguments that the data processing system at issue was an unpatentable "business method." While acknowledging that some authority existed for a "business method" exception to patentable subject matter, the court availed itself of the opportunity to "put this ill-conceived exception to rest." It explained that since the 1952 Patent Act, "business methods have been, and should have been, subject to the same legal requirements for patentability as applied to any other process or method." *State Street,* 149 F.3d at 1375.

Banks, Internet enterprises and other businesses affected by this ruling had not been accustomed to dealing with patents, but the *State Street* decision triggered a surge of patent applications, first for business method-related software, and later for business methods by themselves. Indeed, enterprising lawyers began to patent methods of arbitrating contract disputes and tax avoidance strategies. See, e.g., U.S. Patent No. 6567790 (issued May 20, 2003). Since "business methods" were rarely, if ever, patented in the past, and many business treated their innovative business methods as trade secrets, concern arose that the PTO's search of the prior art (which focuses primarily on prior patents and technical publications) in evaluating business method applications would fail to uncover information relevant to their novelty and non-obviousness. This, in turn, would lead the PTO to grant overly broad, unwarranted patents, with anticompetitive effect.

Many commentators and courts construed the Federal Circuit's decision in *Bilski* as an attempt to cut back significantly on patents for business methods. See, e.g., Cybersource Corp. v. Retail Decisions, Inc., 2009 W.L. 815448 at 9-10 (N.D. Ca. 2009) ("In analyzing *Bilski,* one is led to ponder whether the end has arrived for business method patents * * *. Without expressly overruling *State Street,* the *Bilski* majority struck down its underpinnings. * * * The closing bell may be ringing for business method patents, and their patentees may find they have become bagholders."). What is the likely impact of the *Supreme Court's* decision on the availability of patents for business methods?

Is a limited construction of "process," as advocated by Justice Stevens, consistent with the Court's opinion in *Chakrabarty*? How might one define "business methods?" Is Justice Stevens' distinction between a "process that is useful for conducting business and a claim that merely describes a method of doing business" helpful? As a matter of policy, should business methods be considered patentable subject matter? Will doing so "promote the progress of useful arts"? Why or why not? Other countries have hesitated to follow the United States' lead in granting patents for business methods.

The *Bilski* Court suggests that the Federal Circuit might find ways, consistently with its opinion, to limit the availability of business method patents. Would it be possible to define "abstract ideas" in a manner that would encompass most business methods?

The America Invents Act addresses concerns about business method patents in two ways. First, § 14 effectively excludes "tax strategies" from patentable subject matter by providing that they cannot be deemed novel or non-obvious:

> For purposes of evaluating an invention under section 102 or 103 of title 35, United States Code, any strategy for reducing, avoiding, or deferring tax liability, whether known or unknown at the time of the invention or application for patent, shall be

> deemed insufficient to differentiate a claimed invention from the prior art.

Pub. L. No. 112-29 §14(a), 125 Stat. 327 (2011). Section 14(b) defines "tax liability" as "any liability for a tax under any Federal, State, or local law, or the law of any foreign jurisdiction, including any statute, rule, regulation, or ordinance that levies, imposes, or assesses such tax liability." *Id.* The accompanying House Report explains:

> Inventions that fall within the scope of the provision include those especially suitable for use with tax-favored structures that must meet certain requirements, such as employee benefit plans, tax-exempt organizations, or any other entities that must be structured or operated in a particular manner to obtain certain tax consequences. Thus, the provision applies if the effect of an invention is to aid in satisfying the qualification requirements for the desired tax-favored structure, or to allow for tax reduction, avoidance, or deferral not otherwise automatically available in such entity or structure.

H. Rep. No. 112-98 (Part I), 112th Cong., 1st Sess. 79 (2011). Section 14(c) excludes software that assists individuals to file their income tax returns or that assists them with managing their finances. However, the exclusion does not extend to any part of the software that is related to a tax strategy. H. Rep. No. 112-98, *supra,* at 51-52.

The tax strategy prohibition became effective immediately on the AIA's enactment: September 16, 2011. It applies to any patent application pending on, or filed on or after that date, and to any patent issued on or after that date. Pub. L. No. 112-29 § 14(e), 125 Stat 328 (2011). Why should Congress have singled out tax strategy patents for complete annihilation? According to the House Report accompanying the bill:

> Critics assert that it is not fair to permit patents on techniques used to satisfy a government mandate, such as compliance with the Internal Revenue Code. Tax preparers, lawyers, and planners have a long history of sharing their knowledge regarding how to file returns, plan estates, and advise clients.

> The ability to interpret the tax law and implement such interpretations should remain in the public domain, available to all taxpayers and their advisors.

H.R. Rep. No. 112-98, *supra,* at 51.

The second way the AIA addresses problematic business method patents can be found at § 18, which is entitled, "Transitional Program for Covered Business Method Patents." Section 18 requires the PTO to establish a transitional post-grant review proceeding to review the validity of "covered business method patents." Pub. L. No. 112-29 § 18, 125 Stat. 329 (2011). Persons who have been "charged with" or sued for infringement of a covered business method patent (or their real parties at interest or privies) may file a petition to obtain transitional review of the patent, and request a stay of any related civil infringement action, pending the PTO's completion of the review. The accompanying House Report explains that, in the first years that business patents were granted, "the USPTO lacked a sufficient number of examiners with expertise in the relevant art area," and that "there was a dearth of available prior art to assist examiners as they reviewed business method applications." The transitional review process is meant to redress that problem by permitting a subsequent review with "the best prior art available." H. Rep. No. 112-98 (Part I), $112^{th}$ Cong., $1^{st}$ Sess, 54 (2011). However, if the PTO does not invalidate the patent in the transitional post-grant review, the petitioner will be estopped from asserting invalidity on the same grounds in a judicial procedure or a procedure before the International Trade Commission.

Section 18(d) defines a "covered business method patent" as:

> [A] patent that claims a method or corresponding apparatus for performing data processing or other operations used in the practice, administration, or management of a financial product or service, except that the term does not include patents for technological inventions.

Pub. L. No. 112-29, *supra*, at § 18(d)(1). What does the phrase "or other operations" in the definition refer to? The Senate floor debates demonstrate significant disagreement over the scope of "covered business methods." Consider the statement of Senator Schumer, below:

> Mr. SCHUMER: * * * I would like to elucidate the intent behind the definition of business method patents. Other Members have attempted to suggest a narrow reading of the definition, but these interpretations do not reflect the intent of Congress or the drafters of section 18. For example, in connection with the House vote on the America Invents Act, H.R. 1249, Congressman *Shuster* submitted a statement in the *Record* regarding the definition of a "covered business method patent" in section 18. 157 Cong. Rec. H4497 (daily ed. June 23, 2011)
>
> In the statement, Mr. *Shuster* states: "I would like to place in the record my understanding that the definition of 'covered business method patent` . . . is intended to be narrowly construed to target only those business method patents that are unique to the financial services industry." Mr. *Shuster's* interpretation is incorrect.
>
> Nothing in the America Invents Act limits use of section 18 to banks, insurance companies or other members of the financial services industry. Section 18 does not restrict itself to being used by petitioners whose primary business is financial products or services. Rather, it applies to patents that can apply to financial products or services. Accordingly, the fact that a patent is being used by a company that is not a financial services company does not disqualify the patent from section 18 review. Conversely, given the statutory and regulatory limitations on the activities of financial services companies, if a patent is allegedly being used by a financial services company, the patent will qualify as a "covered business method patent."
>
> The plain meaning of "financial product or service" demonstrates that section 18 is not limited to the financial services industry. At its most basic, a financial product is an agreement between two parties stipulating movements of

money or other consideration now or in the future. Types of financial products include, but are not limited to: extending credit, servicing loans, activities related to extending and accepting credit, leasing of personal or real property, real estate services, appraisals of real or personal property, deposit-taking activities, selling, providing, issuing, or accepting stored value or payment instruments, check cashing, collection or processing, financial data processing, administration and processing of benefits, financial fraud detection and prevention, financial advisory or management consulting services, issuing, selling and trading financial instruments and other securities, insurance products and services, collecting analyzing, maintaining or providing consumer report information or other account information, asset management, trust functions, annuities, securities brokerage, private placement services, investment transactions, and related support services. To be eligible for section 18 review, the patent claims must only be broad enough to cover a financial product or service.

The definition of "covered business method patent" also indicates that the patent must relate to "performing data processing or other operations used in the practice, administration, or management" of a financial product or service. This language makes it clear that section 18 is intended to cover not only patents claiming the financial product or service itself, but also patents claiming activities that are financial in nature, incidental to a financial activity or complementary to a financial activity. Any business that sells or purchases goods or services "practices" or "administers" a financial service by conducting such transactions. * * *

* * *

Moreover, the text of section 18 further demonstrates that section 18 is not limited to patents exclusively utilized by the financial services industry. As originally adopted in the Senate, subsection (a)(1)(B) only allowed a party to file a section 18 petition if either that party or its real parties in interest had been sued or accused of infringement. In the

House, this was expanded to also cover cases where a "privy" of the petitioner had been sued or accused of infringement. A "privy" is a party that has a direct relationship to the petitioner with respect to the allegedly infringing product or service. In this case, it effectively means customers of the petitioner. With the addition of the word "privy," a company could seek a section 18 proceeding on the basis that customers of the petitioner had been sued for infringement. Thus, the addition of the "privy" language clearly demonstrates that section 18 applies to patents that may be used by entities other than the financial services industry.

The fact that a multitude of industries will be able to make use of section [18] is evident by the broad based support for the provision, including the U.S. Chamber of Commerce and the National Retail Federation, among many others.

157 Cong. Rec. S5432 (daily ed. Sept. 8, 2011)(statement of Senator Schumer). Compare the statement of Senator Leahy, after whom the Act is named:

Mr. LEAHY: * * * There has been some question about the scope of patents that may be subject to the transitional program for covered business method patents * * * This provision is intended to cover only those business method patents intended to be used in the practice, administration, or management of financial services or products, and not to technologies common in business environments across sectors and that have no particular relation to the financial services sector, such as computers, communications networks, and business software.

A financial product or service is not, however, intended to be limited solely to the operation of banks. Rather, it is intended to have a broader industry definition that includes insurance, brokerages, mutual funds, annuities and an array of financial companies outside of traditional banking.

157 Cong. Rec. S5441 (daily ed. Sept. 8, 2011)(statement of Senator Leahy).

There is likely also to be some dispute about what constitutes an excluded "technological invention." How would you define it? Consider the statement of Senator Coburn, below:

> Mr. COBURN: * * * I understand that section 18 will not make all business method patents subject to review by the U.S. Patent and Trademark Office. Rather, section 18 is designed to address the problem of low-quality business patents that are commonly associated with the Federal Circuit's 1998 *State Street* decision. I further understand that section 18 of the bill specifically exempts "patents for technological inventions" from this new review at USPTO.
>
> Patents for technological inventions are those patents whose novelty turns on a technological innovation over the prior art and are concerned with a technical problem which is solved with a technical solution. The technological innovation exception does not exclude a patent from section 18 simply because it recites technology. Inventions related to manufacturing and machines that do not simply use known technology to accomplish a novel business process would be excluded from review under section 18.
>
> For example, section 18 would not cover patents related to the manufacture and distribution of machinery to count, sort, and authenticate currency. It is the intention of section 18 to not review mechanical inventions related to the manufacture and distribution of machinery to count, sort, and authenticate currency like change sorters and machines that scan paper instruments, including currency, whose novelty turns on a technological innovation over the prior art. * * *

157 Cong. Rec. S5428 (daily ed. Sept. 8, 2011)(statement of Senator Coburn). How helpful is this explanation? The AIA instructs the PTO to issue regulations for determining whether a patented invention is a

"technological invention." Pub. L. No. 112-29 § 18(d)(2), 125 Stat. 331 (2011).

All "covered business method patents" are subject to the transitional post-grant review, regardless of whether they issued before or after enactment of the America Invents Act. The review procedure becomes available on September 16, 2012, and sunsets eight years later. Pub. L. No. 112-29, *supra,* § 18 (a)(3).

4. *Computer programs and mathematical algorithms.* In determining that the *Bilski* method constituted an unpatentable abstract idea, the Supreme Court relied heavily on *Gottschalk v. Benson, Parker v. Flook,* and *Diamond v. Diehr*, all of which involved claims to software, or mathematical algorithms. (These cases are sometimes called the Court's "software trilogy.") *Benson* held that mathematical algorithms (of which computer programs are comprised) are unpatentable abstract ideas. *Flook* took "the next logical step," and held that the prohibition against patenting abstract ideas could not be circumvented by attempting to limit the use of the algorithm to a particular technological environment or adding insignificant post-solution activity. *Diehr* limited the principles stated in *Benson* and *Flook* by holding that "an application of a law of nature or mathematical formula to a known structure or process may well be deserving of patent protection." Thus, claiming a mathematical algorithm as one element of a process, machine or article of manufacture does not necessarily preclude a patent. In *Diehr,* the Supreme Court found a that a claimed process for curing synthetic rubber, which combined well-known rubber-curing steps with use of a programmed computer (which repeatedly recalculated the necessary cure time given variables in mold temperature) constituted patentable subject matter. The Court explained that granting a patent on the process would not give a monopoly in the mathematical algorithm with which the computer was programmed—it would only give rights in the use of the algorithm in combination with the other claimed process steps. Thus the patentee claimed a specific application of the abstract idea, not the abstract idea itself.

In *In re* Alappat, 33 F.3d 1526 (Fed.Cir.1994), the claimed invention improved the ability of a finite pixel cathode-ray tube (a visual screen like that of a television) to show a smooth diagonal line. Because the visual screen has only a fixed number of pixels, or illumination points, which are all the same size, its display of strongly sloped lines may appear jagged. Alappat's invention alleviated the problem by varying the illumination intensity of each pixel according to an anti-aliasing algorithm (a mathematical formula). Essentially, Alappat's invention operated on one set of numbers (vector list data) and produced another set of numbers (pixel illumination intensity data). Alappat disclosed "hard-wired" logic circuitry to perform the algorithm, but drafted his claims in a manner that would encompass any general-purpose computer programmed to perform the algorithm. The PTO denied a patent under Patent Act § 101, on the ground that the application merely claimed a mathematical algorithm. In a controversial *en banc* decision that produced seven separate opinions, the Court of Appeals for the Federal Circuit found that the application stated patentable subject matter.

The majority reasoned that because the claims encompassed structural elements (computer hardware), the claimed invention constituted a "machine," which is statutory subject matter. The Federal Circuit characterized the "mathematical algorithm" exception to patentability as a very narrow exception that applies only in cases in which the claim, as a whole, is to a disembodied mathematical concept, representing nothing more than a law of nature, natural phenomenon, or abstract idea. If, as in *Alappat*, the claim makes a practical application of the mathematical concept, then the exception should not apply. The majority dismissed the objection that the claims in that case were so broad that they would extend to any general-purpose computer programmed to carry out the same algorithm. The majority noted that the programming "creates a new machine, because a general purpose computer in effect becomes a special purpose computer once it is programmed to perform particular functions pursuant to instructions from program software." Thus, a claim for a known, general-purpose computer in combination with a new mathematical algorithm constitutes a claim for a new machine, and patentable subject matter.

The dissent characterized the applicant's claim as having "no substance apart from the calculations involved," and argued that the majority's reasoning elevated form over substance: All that Alappat really claimed to have discovered was a mathematical algorithm, which is unpatentable subject matter. Drafting his claim to include computer hardware was a subterfuge that did not change the essence of the claim. The practical effect of the majority's reading of the claim was to grant a patent in an abstract idea or law of nature. The dissent also rejected the notion that a computer constitutes a new machine each time a new program is loaded into it, questioning the logic of basing a finding of "newness" for purposes of patentability on a difference that is strictly unpatentable in itself.

How would Alappat's claim fare in light of the Supreme Court's more recent decisions in *Bilski* and *Mayo*? Do those cases dictate a different outcome? Why or why not?

Patents have also been granted for claims to software elements stored in a memory device, such as a disk or chip. See *In re* Lowry, 32 F.3d 1579 (Fed.Cir.1994); U.S. Patent & Trademark Office, *Examination Guidelines for Computer–Related Inventions*, 61 Fed. Reg. 7478 (1996). In such cases, the claims are deemed to fall into the "article of manufacture" category of patentable subject matter, because when software is recorded on a computer-readable medium it becomes "structurally and functionally interrelated to the medium," which permits the computer program's functionality to be realized. *Id.* at 7481. However, in CyberSource Corp. v. Retail Decisions, Inc, 654 F.3d 1366 (Fed. Cir. 2011), the Federal Circuit rejected an "article of manufacture" claim to a computer readable medium containing program instructions to carry out a process, because the process itself did not constitute patentable subject matter.

In that case, claim 3 claimed a method for verifying the validity of a credit card transaction over the Internet, using "Internet address" information (IP addresses, MAC addresses, e-mail addresses, etc.) to determine whether an Internet address relating to a particular transaction is consistent with other Internet addresses that have been used in transactions involving the same credit card. The claim was comprised of three steps: a) obtaining information about other transactions that have utilized an Internet address that is identified with the credit card transaction; b) constructing a map of credit card numbers based upon the other transactions and; c) utilizing the map of credit card numbers to determine if the credit card transaction is valid. The Federal Circuit noted that the method "simply require[d] one to 'obtain and compare intangible data pertinent to business risks,'" and neither transformed matter nor involved use of a machine. *Id.,* 654 F.3d. at 1370. Rather, the claim was drawn to an "unpatentable mental process," which the court described as a subcategory of unpatentable abstract ideas. The court cited *Gottschalk v. Benson* for the proposition that "methods which can be performed mentally, or which are the equivalent of human mental work, are unpatentable abstract ideas—the 'basic tools of scientific and technological work' that are open to all." *Cybersource, supra,* 654 F.3d at 1371-73 (citing *Benson, supra,* 409 U.S. at 67).

Turning to claim 2 (the "Beauregard," or article of manufacture claim), the Federal Circuit noted:

> [W]e found claim 3 to be unpatentable because it is drawn to a mental process—i.e., an abstract idea. The method underlying claim 2 is clearly the same method of fraud detection recited in claim 3. Nonetheless, CyberSource contends that claim 2 should be patentable. CyberSource's main argument is that coupling the unpatentable mental process recited in claim 3 with a manufacture or machine renders it patent-eligible.
>
> CyberSource argues that claim 2 is patent-eligible per se because it recites a "manufacture," rather than a "process," under the statutory language of § 101. CyberSource contends that, by definition, a tangible, man-made article of manufacture such as a "computer readable medium containing program instructions" cannot possibly fall within any of the three patent-eligibility exceptions the Supreme Court has recognized for "laws of nature, physical phenomena, [or] abstract ideas." We disagree.
>
> Regardless of what statutory category ("process, machine, manufacture, or composition of matter,") a claim's language is crafted to literally invoke, we look to the underlying invention for patent-eligibility purposes. Here, it is

> clear that the invention underlying both claims 2 and 3 is a method for detecting credit card fraud, not a manufacture for storing computer-readable information. * * *
>
> In the present case, CyberSource has not met its burden to demonstrate that claim 2 is "truly drawn to a specific" computer readable medium, rather than to the underlying method of credit fraud detection. To be sure, * * * we have held that, as a general matter, programming a general purpose computer to perform an algorithm "creates a new machine, because a general purpose computer in effect becomes a special purpose computer once it is programmed to perform particular functions pursuant to instructions from program software." *In re Alappat,* 33 F.3d 1526, 1545 (Fed. Cir. 1994). But we have never suggested that simply reciting the use of a computer to execute an algorithm that can be performed entirely in the human mind falls within the *Alappat* rule. Thus, despite its Beauregard claim format, * * * we treat claim 2 as a process claim for patent-eligibility purposes.

*Id.,* at 1374-75.

In *CLS Bank International v. Alice Corp. PTY. Ltd.,* __ F.3d __, 2013 W.L. 1920941 (2013), the Federal Circuit, sitting *en banc,* undertook to state a rationale for analyzing the abstract idea exception in cases involving computer-implemented method, storage media, and system claims, in light of *Bilski* and *Mayo.* The four patents before it concerned a form of computerized escrow to reduce the risk in financial transactions: "a computerized trading platform used for conducting financial transactions in which a third party settles obligations between a first and a second party so as to eliminate 'counterparty' or 'settlement" risk'—the 'risk to each party in an exchange that only one of the two parties will actually pay its obligation, leaving the paying party without its principal or the benefit of the counterparty's performance.' __ F.3d at __, 2013 W.L. 1920941 at 1. The court asked for briefing on two questions:

> 1. What test should the court adopt to determine whether a computer-implemented invention is a patent ineligible "abstract

idea"; and when, if ever, does the presence of a computer in a claim lend patent eligibility to an otherwise patent-ineligible idea?

2. In assessing patent eligibility under 35 U.S.C. § 101 of a computer-implemented invention, should it matter whether the invention is claimed as a method, system, or storage medium; and should such claims at times be considered equivalent for § 101 purposes?

The court fractured in its attempt to address these questions. It produced a one-paragraph *per curiam* opinion invalidating the computer method and computer-readable medium claims before it, and split 5-5 over the patent eligibility of the computer system claims. Various members of the court wrote or joined 6 different opinions concurring or dissenting or dissenting in part with the result, but these widely varying opinions provided little guidance or precedent for future cases. One of the important points of contention in the various opinions was the continuing relevance of the *Alapatt* decision (discussed *supra*) after the Supreme Court's decisions in *Bilski* and *Mayo*.

5. *In re Nuijten.* In *In re* Nuijten, 500 F.3d 1346 (Fed. Cir. 2007), the applicant developed a method of reducing the distortion that watermarking created in transitory signals. The applicant was able to patent his process for encoding signals to reduce distortion, a device to perform the process, and a storage medium to hold the encoded signals. However, the Federal Circuit rejected his claims to the encoded signals themselves.[6] The court reasoned that the signals, as claimed, failed to fall into any of the section 101 categories of patentable subject matter.

---

6 The independent claim at issue stated:

> A signal with embedded supplemental data, the signal being encoded in accordance with a given encoding process and selected samples of the signal representing the supplemental data, and at least one of the samples preceding the selected samples is different from the sample corresponding to the given encoding process.

The ensuing dependent claims added requirements that the embedded data be a watermark, that the signal be a video signal, and that the signal be an audio signal. *In re Nuijten*, 500 F.3d at 1351.

The claims anticipated that the data would be embedded in some physical carrier, such as modulated electromagnetic waves, electrical signals, or pulses in fiber optic cables, though they did not limit the signals to any particular physical form. The court thus characterized the claims as describing "physical but transitory forms of signal transmission such as radio broadcasts, electrical signals through a wire, and light pulses through a fiber-optic cable, as long as those transmissions convey information encoded in the manner disclosed and claimed." *Id.*, at 1353.

The court held that the signals did not constitute a "process," because a process entails an act or series of acts. The signal claims did not call for any action, but merely claimed the product of action. *Id.*, at 1355. Nor were the signals "machines" within the meaning of section 101. The court defined a machine as "a concrete thing, consisting of parts, or of certain devices," a "mechanical device or combination of mechanical powers and devices to perform some function and produce a certain effect or result." *Id.*, at 1355. However, a "transitory signal made of electrical or electromagnetic variances is not made of 'parts' or 'devices' in any mechanical sense. While such a signal is physical and real, it does not possess concrete structure in the sense implied by these definitions." *Id.*

The court found the question of whether the signals constituted "manufactures" (or "articles of manufacture") more difficult, because they were man-made. However, it found that artificiality was insufficient by itself to render something an article of manufacture. Rather, Supreme Court precedent defined a section 101 "manufacture" as a tangible article or commodity.

> A transient electric or electromagnetic transmission does not fit within that definition. While such a transmission is man-made and physical–it exists in the real world and has tangible causes and effects–it is a change in electric potential that, to be perceived must be measured at a certain point in space and time by equipment capable of detecting and interpreting the signal. In essence, energy embodying the claimed signal is fleeting and is devoid of any semblance of permanence during

> transmission. Moreover, any tangibility arguably attributed to a signal is embodied in the principle that it is perceptible–e.g., changes in electrical potential can be measured. All signals within the scope of the claim do not themselves comprise some tangible article or commodity. This is particularly true when the signal is encoded on an electromagnetic carrier and transmitted through a vacuum--a medium that, by definition, is devoid of matter. Thus, we hold that Nuijten's signals, standing alone, are not "manufacture[s]" within the meaning of that term in § 101.

*Id.*, at 1356-57.

Finally, the court held that since the signals were not "composed of matter," they could not be deemed "compositions of matter" for purposes of § 101. Accordingly, the signals did not fall into any of the section 101 categories of patentable subject matter, and the claims must be rejected.

Do you find the court's reasoning compelling? In this modern age, why should "manufactures" be limited to tangible things? Shouldn't statutory subject matter be construed broadly, to cover the full scope of technological ingenuity? Could the signals be deemed laws of nature, natural phenomena, or abstract ideas?

6. *Patents for new uses of old products*. Patent Act § 100 provides that the term "process" "includes a new use of a known process, machine, manufacture, composition of matter or material." Thus, for example, a person who discovers that a known chemical compound has previously unknown medicinal qualities may obtain a patent on the process of treating patients with the compound, assuming that the other requirements of the Patent Act are satisfied. As the Supreme Court has explained, this type of "process" patent is particularly important to inventors in chemical research:

> The number of chemicals either known to scientists or disclosed by existing research is vast. It grows constantly, as those engaging in "pure" research publish their discoveries. The number of these chemicals that have known uses of

> commercial or social value, in contrast, is small. Development of new uses for existing chemicals is thus a major component of practical chemical research. It may take years of unsuccessful testing before a chemical having a desired property is identified, and it may take several years of further testing before a proper and safe method for using that chemical is developed.

Dawson Chemical Co. v. Rohm & Haas Co., 448 U.S. 176, 221–22, 100 S.Ct. 2601, 2626, 65 L.Ed.2d 696, 718 (1980).

7. *Medical procedure patents*. Many countries limit the availability of patents for medical or surgical procedures on ethical or social policy grounds. It has been argued that issuance of medical procedure patents may chill doctors' free use of the best and latest available techniques in treating patients. Moreover, the availability of patents may inhibit the customary sharing of information in the field and add to the expense of health care. It has also been asserted that medical procedure patents are not needed because most discoveries are made in the course of doctors' practice, do not depend on capital investment, and are not needed as an incentive to invent. See generally *Medical Procedures Innovation and Affordability Act & Inventor Protection Act of 1995: Hearings on H.R. 1127 and H.R. 2419 Before the Subcomm. on Courts and Intellectual Property of the House Comm. on the Judiciary,* 104th Cong., 1st Sess. (1995).

Unlike other countries, the United States has not excepted any category of medical or surgical procedures from patentable subject matter. Most U.S. medical process patents are directed to methods of using medical devices and pharmaceuticals, which may also be patented. These patents can be contrasted with patents for medical or diagnostic procedures, such as the Heimlich maneuver or CPR, which do not center on the use of chemical compounds or innovative medical devices. Although the PTO has issued patents for medical procedure inventions in the latter category, most of these have never been enforced. Rather, doctors traditionally have obtained them primarily as a means of claiming credit for their discoveries, with no expectation of a direct financial reward.

These patents became controversial in the 1990's when a doctor undertook to enforce a patent that he had obtained for a method of stitchless cataract surgery, which uses the internal pressure of the eye to seal a tunnel-like incision. The patentee brought an infringement suit against the Dartmouth–Hitchcock Clinic and a Vermont doctor who had been using and teaching the technique. He sought to enjoin unauthorized use and impose a royalty of $5 per use. The patentee's lawyers estimated that approximately one-third of the 10,000 U.S. ophthalmic surgeons used the technique. See 52 Pat. Trademark & Copyright J. 44 (BNA)(1996). At around the same time, a California obstetrician decided to enforce his patent on a method for determining the sex of a fetus through ultrasound, and Yale University stated its intention to enforce a patent on a method of detecting breast cancer tumors by examining tissue for Tamoxifen metabolites. 49 Pat. Trademark & Copyright J. 530–31 (BNA)(1995). The American Medical Association's and others' objections to these developments led to the introduction of bills in Congress to prevent the issuance of patents for such medical or diagnostic procedures, or to limit their enforcement.

Congress' solution ultimately was not to exclude any medical procedures from the subject matter of patents. To exclude them would have been inconsistent with the position the U.S. had taken in international patent negotiations, advocating that patents should be available for all fields of technology. Rather, Congress amended Patent Act § 287 to prohibit infringement remedies against certain persons—medical practitioners and related health care entities—who directly infringe or induce infringement of a patent through performance of a "medical activity." The term, "medical activity," is defined as "the performance of a medical or surgical procedure on a body." 35 U.S.C. § 287(c)(2)(A). There are, however, several very important exceptions: infringement remedies remain available if the medical practitioner (1) makes unauthorized use of a patented machine, article of manufacture, or composition of matter; (2) practices a patented method of administering a composition of matter without authorization; or (3) practices a patented biotechnology process without authorization. Thus, the § 287(c) limitation is a rather narrow one, which applies primarily when the infringed patent claims a surgical or medical procedure that does not involve drugs as an important component, or patented devices. Even then, indirect infringement remedies (for inducing or contributing to the direct infringement) may be available to the patentee under certain circumstances.

Was Congress' response adequate? What arguments can be made in support of fully enforceable patents for all medical and diagnostic procedures?

## C. STANDARDS OF PATENTABILITY

* * *

### 2. Section 102: Novelty
### 3. Section 102: The Statutory Bar

*Pages 169-201--Replace 2. Section 102: Novelty, and 3. Section 102: The Statutory Bar, with the following:*

### 2. Section 102: Novelty and the Statutory Bar

When two different inventors make the same invention, which one gets the patent? The world norm is to grant the patent to the first inventor to file an application. However, the United States has traditionally preferred to grant a patent to the first person to make the invention. The Leahy-Smith America Invents Act moves the United States from its singular "first-to-invent" priority system to a "first inventor to file" system, and makes a range of changes to the "novelty" and "statutory bar" provisions of Patent Act §102 in order to implement it. These changes become effective on March 16, 2013, and apply to patent applications with effective filing dates on or after that date. This represents a highly significant and controversial change. Since the pre-AIA "novelty," and "statutory bar" provisions will continue to apply to all applications until the effective date, and will continue to govern the validity of patents granted on earlier applications, it will be important for students to be familiar with both the old and the new § 102 provisions. Accordingly, this section will discuss the pre-AIA novelty and statutory provisions in subpart a, *supra,* pre-AIA statutory bar provisions in subpart b, *supra,* and the new AIA priority and novelty provisions in subpart c, *supra.*

### a. The Pre-America Invents Act Novelty Provisions

As noted above, the United States has traditionally granted a patent to the first person to invent. Patent Act sections 102(a), (e), and (g) work together to make it very difficult for a "subsequent inventor" to obtain a patent. Section 102(a) provides that an applicant will be denied a patent if, prior to the applicant's invention date: the invention was "known" in the United States; the invention was "used" in the United States; the invention was the subject of a patent anywhere in the world; or the invention was revealed in a "printed publication" anywhere in the world. Section 102(e) provides that even if the earlier invention was not disclosed to the public in any of the ways enumerated in subsection (a), its existence will preclude the subsequent inventor from obtaining a patent if it was disclosed in a U.S. patent application that was pending on the subsequent inventor's invention date and was later published under §122(b) or granted. Section 102(g) places a final obstacle in the subsequent inventor's path to the Patent Office. Under subsection (g), the applicant will be denied a patent if: (1) prior to the applicant's invention date, another person made the invention in the U.S. and had not abandoned, suppressed or concealed it; or (2) another person has established in an interference action that he made the invention abroad prior to the applicant's invention date and has not abandoned, suppressed or concealed it.[1]

---

[1] A patent interference is a proceeding in the PTO to determine which claimant is the earlier inventor when there are conflicting claims. The PTO may declare an interference between pending applications or between an issued patent and an application, when each claims substantially the same invention.

As you can see, subsections 102(a), (e) and (g) all focus on the applicant's invention date. The act of invention consists of two parts: 1) conception, and 2) reduction to practice. An inventor conceives of the invention when he formulates a definite, complete idea of the operative invention, so that all that remains is the physical realization of it. The mental concept must be complete to the point that a person with ordinary skill in the art could then produce it without further invention.[2] The inventor may reduce the concept to practice in either of two ways. She may perform an *actual reduction to practice* by building a physical prototype of the invention (or in the case of a process, by actually carrying out the steps of the process) and ascertaining that it works for the intended purpose. The inventor may *constructively reduce the invention to practice* by filing a patent application that fully discloses the invention. It is presumed that the first person to reduce the invention to practice is the first to invent. However, a person making a later reduction to practice may rebut that presumption by showing that she was the *first to conceive* of the invention and was *reasonably diligent in reducing it to practice* from a date prior to the conception date of the first to reduce to practice.

NetMoneyIn, Inc. v. Verisign, Inc., below, explains when a publication made prior to the applicant's invention date will "anticipate" the applicant's invention, rendering it non-novel and unpatentable under § 102(a). The following notes explore more fully how § 102(a), (e) and (g) work.

## NET MONEYIN, INC. v. VERISIGN, INC.

United States Court of Appeals for the Federal Circuit, 2008.
545 F.3d 1359.

---

[2] The inventor must not only conceive of the invention, but also understand his creation to have the features comprising the inventive subject matter. An accidental invention, in which the prior inventor does not recognize or appreciate the invention's innovative qualities, does not anticipate a later one. See Invitrogen Corp. v. Clontech Laboratories, Inc., 429 F.3d 1052, 1063-66 (Fed. Cir. 2005).

LINN, Circuit Judge.

Net MoneyIN, Inc. ("NMI") appeals from a final judgment of the United States District Court for the District of Arizona, which held the asserted claims of U.S. Patents No. 5,822,737 ("the '737 patent") and No. 5,963,917 ("the '917 patent") invalid. * * * Because the district court applied an incorrect standard of law in finding claim 23 of the '737 patent invalid as anticipated under 35 U.S.C. § 102(a), * * * we reverse the grant of summary judgment of anticipation. * * *

I. BACKGROUND

This case involves systems for processing credit card transactions over the Internet and for addressing security concerns not present in direct retail transactions. In the early days of Internet commerce, merchants recognized that one key to the success of Internet sales would be the ability to provide customers with assurances of security in the processing of financial transactions over the Internet using credit cards, bank accounts, and other means of electronic payment. Responding to that need, the industry investigated encryption techniques and architectures to protect sensitive data. One such effort is reflected in a 1995 working document entitled "Internet Keyed Payments Protocol" ("the IKP reference"), published by the Internet Engineering Task Force and IBM. That document sets forth standards on "how payments may be accomplished efficiently, reliably[,] and securely." The IKP reference explains that its goal was "to enable Internet-based secure electronic payments while utilizing the existing financial infrastructure for payment authorization and clearance. The intent is to avoid completely, or at least minimize, changes to the existing financial infrastructure outside the Internet." To that end, the IKP reference suggests two standard models, or protocols.

In the first protocol, (1) the customer selects one or more items to purchase from the merchant's website; (2) the customer sends credit card information to the merchant; (3) the merchant sends the credit card information and amount of the purchase to the merchant's bank; (4) the merchant's bank seeks authorization for the purchase from the issuing bank over the existing banking network; and (5) the merchant's bank notifies the merchant (but not the customer) of transaction approval.

In the second protocol, (1) the customer selects one or more items to purchase on the merchant's website; (2) the customer sends an authorization request, along with its credit card information and the amount of the purchase, to the merchant's bank; (3) the merchant's bank seeks authorization from the issuing bank over the existing banking network; (4) the merchant's bank notifies the customer of transaction approval; and (5) the customer sends the authorization response to the merchant.

Unsatisfied with the early approaches taken by others, Mark Ogram, an inventor and patent attorney, set out to create a new payment model to remedy what he perceived as two deficiencies in the prior art protocols: "the fact that the customer had to send confidential information over the Internet to an unknown merchant; and the fact that credit card issuers imposed onerous financial requirements on merchants." Ogram's idea was to add a fifth entity, a "payment processing" or "financial processing" entity, to supplement the conventional model with four entities: the customer, merchant, merchant's bank, and issuing bank. According to Ogram, the new financial processing entity would: "(1) receive credit card account information and an amount to be charged from the customer when the customer placed the order; (2) seek authorization from the card issuer over the existing banking network; and (3) notify both the customer and the merchant of authorization."

On February 5, 1996, Ogram filed a patent application directed to a payment model utilizing a financial processing entity. He formed NMI shortly thereafter to implement the model as a business for processing credit card transactions over the Internet. Ogram's patent application resulted in the '737 and '917 patents, both of which are assigned to NMI. Claim 1 of the '737 patent is illustrative of the invention claimed:

1. A financial transaction system comprising:

a) a first bank computer containing financial data therein, said financial data including customer account numbers and available credit data, said first bank computer including means for generating an authorization indicia in response to queries containing a customer account number and amount;

b) a merchant computer containing promotional data;

c) a customer computer being linked with said merchant computer and receiving said promotional data; and,

d) a financial processing computer remote from said merchant computer and having means for:

1) receiving customer account data and amount data from said customer computer,

2) querying said first bank computer with said customer account data and said amount data,

3) receiving an authorization indicia from said first bank computer,

4) communicating a self-generated transaction indicia to said customer computer, and,

5) communicating the self-generated transaction indicia to said merchant computer.

According to their abstracts, the '737 and '917 patents relate to “[a]n automated payment system particularly suited for purchases over a distributed computer network such as the Internet.”

In 2001, NMI filed suit for infringement of the '737 and '917 patents against a number of parties alleged to compete in the Internet credit card processing field, including VeriSign, Inc. and eProcessing Network (collectively, “VeriSign”). * * *

* * * VeriSign moved for summary judgment of invalidity, arguing that the IKP reference anticipated claim 23 of the '737 patent under 35 U.S.C. § 102(a). The district court granted VeriSign's motion. * * *

II. DISCUSSION

* * *

2. Anticipation

Claim 23 of the '737 patent recites an Internet payment system comprising five "links":

> [1] a first link between a customer computer and a vending computer for communicating promotional information from said vending computer to said customer computer;
>
> [2] a second link, initiated by said customer computer, between said customer computer and a payment processing computer, remote from said vending computer, for communicating credit card information and amount from said customer computer to said payment processing computer;
>
> [3] a third link, initiated by said payment processing computer with a credit card server computer for communicating said credit card information and said amount from said payment processing computer to said credit card server computer, and for communicating, in response, an authorization indicia from said credit card server computer to said payment processing computer; [ ]
>
> [4] a fourth link between said payment processing computer and said customer computer for communicating a transactional indicia[;]
>
> [5] a fifth link between the payment processing computer and said vending computer for communicating said transactional indicia.

The district court, after finding all five of these links in the IKP reference, albeit in two separate disclosed examples, concluded that claim 23 was anticipated under 35 U.S.C. § 102(a) and therefore invalid. Specifically, the district court concluded:

> All of the limitations of claim 23 can be found within the IKP reference. A simple combination would produce the system described in claim 23 of the '737 patent. That no specific example within IKP contains all five links does not preclude a finding of anticipation.

NMI contends that the district court's combination of two disclosed examples in order to find all elements of the claim was erroneous. VeriSign responds that the district court did not improperly rearrange the links in the IKP reference, but rather "merely relied on various express teachings from a single document that together completely disclose the five claimed links." Under VeriSign's theory, this was sufficient to establish anticipation, because all that is required is "that the four corners of a single, prior art document describe every element of the claimed invention." We disagree with VeriSign, and take this opportunity to clarify what a reference must show in order to anticipate a claimed invention.

Section 102(a) provides that an issued patent is invalid if "the invention [therein] was ... described in a printed publication ... before the invention thereof by the applicant." Section 102 embodies the concept of novelty--if a device or process has been previously invented (and disclosed to the public), then it is not new, and therefore the claimed invention is "anticipated" by the prior invention. As we have stated numerous times (language on which VeriSign relies), in order to demonstrate anticipation, the proponent must show "that the four corners of a single, prior art document describe every element of the claimed invention." This statement embodies the requirement in section 102 that the anticipating invention be "described in a printed publication," and is, of course, unimpeachable. But it does not tell the whole story. Because the hallmark of anticipation is prior invention, the prior art reference--in order to anticipate under 35 U.S.C. § 102--must not only disclose all elements of the claim within the four corners of the document, but must also disclose those elements "arranged as in the claim." *Connell v. Sears, Roebuck & Co.,* 722 F.2d 1542, 1548 (Fed.Cir.1983).

The meaning of the expression "arranged as in the claim" is readily understood in relation to claims drawn to things such as ingredients mixed in some claimed order. In such instances, a reference that discloses all of the claimed ingredients, but not in the order claimed, would not anticipate, because the reference would be missing any disclosure of the limitations of the claimed invention "arranged as in the claim." But the "arranged as in the claim" requirement is not limited to such a narrow set of "order of limitations" claims. Rather, our precedent informs that the "arranged as in the claim" requirement applies to all claims and refers to the need for an anticipatory reference to show all of the limitations of the claims arranged or combined in the same way as recited in the claims, not merely in a particular order. The test is thus more accurately understood to mean "arranged or combined in the same way as in the claim."

For example, in *Lindemann Maschinenfabrik GMBH v. American Hoist & Derrick Co.,* 730 F.2d 1452 (Fed.Cir.1984), we reviewed a district court's determination that a patent directed to a hydraulic scrap shearing machine was anticipated by a prior patent directed to a method for shearing spent nuclear fuel bundles. Because the district court had "treated the claims as mere catalogs of separate parts, in disregard of the part-to-part relationships set forth in the claims and that give the claims their meaning," we reversed. Although the prior art reference could be said to contain all of the elements of the claimed invention, it did not anticipate under 35 U.S.C. § 102 because it "disclose[d] an entirely different device, composed of parts distinct from those of the claimed invention, and operating in a different way to process different material differently." *Id.* at 1458. The reference thus was deficient because it did not disclose the elements of the claimed invention "arranged as in the claim" as required by 35 U.S.C. § 102.

* * *

* * * We thus hold that unless a reference discloses within the four corners of the document not only all of the limitations claimed but

also all of the limitations arranged or combined in the same way as recited in the claim, it cannot be said to prove prior invention of the thing claimed and, thus, cannot anticipate under 35 U.S.C. § 102.

Here, the IKP reference discloses two separate protocols for processing an Internet credit card transaction. Neither of these protocols contains all five links arranged or combined in the same way as claimed in the '737 patent. Thus, although the IKP reference might anticipate a claim directed to either of the two protocols disclosed, it cannot anticipate the system of claim 23. The district court was wrong to conclude otherwise.

The district court was also wrong to combine parts of the separate protocols shown in the IKP reference in concluding that claim 23 was anticipated. Granted, there may be only slight differences between the protocols disclosed in the IKP reference and the system of claim 23. But differences between the prior art reference and a claimed invention, however slight, invoke the question of obviousness, not anticipation. *See* 35 U.S.C. § 103(a) ("A patent may not be obtained though the invention is not *identically* disclosed or described as set forth in section 102 of this title, if the differences between the subject matter sought to be patented and the prior art are such that the subject matter as a whole would have been obvious at the time the invention was made to a person having ordinary skill in the art to which said subject matter pertains." (emphasis added)) * * *. Thus, it is not enough that the prior art reference discloses part of the claimed invention, which an ordinary artisan might supplement to make the whole, or that it includes multiple, distinct teachings that the artisan might somehow combine to achieve the claimed invention. *See In re Arkley,* 455 F.2d 586, 587 (C.C.P.A. 1972) ("[T]he [prior art] reference must clearly and unequivocally disclose the claimed [invention] or direct those skilled in the art to the [invention] without *any* need for picking, choosing, and combining various disclosures not directly related to each other by the teachings of the cited reference.").

Because the parties do not contend that the IKP reference discloses all of the limitations recited in claim [23] arranged or combined in the same way as in the claim, and because it was error for the district court to find anticipation by combining different parts of the separate protocols in the IKP reference simply because they were found within the four corners of the document, we reverse the district court's grant of summary judgment of invalidity.

* * *

### *Notes and Questions*

1. *Identity of invention.* As demonstrated in *Verisign,* lack of novelty ("anticipation") under Patent Act §102 entails "the presence in a single prior art disclosure of all elements of a claimed invention arranged as in that claim." Connell v. Sears, Roebuck and Co., 722 F.2d 1542, 1548 (Fed.Cir.1983). Generally, an anticipating reference--for example, an earlier patent or publication--will expressly disclose all the elements of the later claimed invention. However, the courts have recognized "inherent anticipation," in which the reference does not expressly disclose all the elements of the later invention, but the non-express elements are nonetheless necessarily present in the thing described or disclosed in the reference.[3]

The novelty, statutory bar, and obviousness determinations are all made with reference to the prior art--earlier inventions, patents, and publications as described in § 102. However, while the obviousness determination may be made by combining two or more prior art references, § 102 anticipation requires that the invention be revealed (expressly or inherently) in a single reference--a single earlier invention, patent or publication. Essentially, the test for anticipation is the same as that for literal infringement. If something disclosed in a single reference would have literally infringed the patent if it arose after the patent became effective, then it will anticipate if it arose before the applicant's invention.

---

[3]For a useful discussion of the circumstances in which courts will find that an element is "inherent" in a disclosure, even though not expressly described, see Dan L. Burk and Mark A. Lemley, *Inherency*, 47 Wm. & Mary L. Rev. 371 (2005).

2. *Section 102(a).* Section 102(a) sets forth four different types of disclosure (or "prior art") that will anticipate a later invention and thus render it unpatentable.

*a) The invention was known by others in this country prior to the applicant's invention.* In Application of Borst, 345 F.2d 851 (C.C.P.A.1965), *cert. denied,* 382 U.S. 973 (1966), the Court of Customs and Patent Appeals set forth two requirements that must be satisfied in order to demonstrate that an invention was "known" prior to the applicant's invention, within the meaning of §102(a). First, the invention must have been fully disclosed. Second, the invention must have been accessible to the public. *Id.*, 345 F.2d at 854.

With regard to the "fully disclosed" requirement, prior case law had held that in order to anticipate, an earlier invention must have been either actually or constructively reduced to practice. As noted *supra*, actual reduction to practice entails making a physical embodiment of the invention (or in the case of a process, carrying out the steps of the process) and ascertaining that the invention works for the intended purpose. Constructive reduction to practice entails filing a patent application for the invention. The *Borst* court reasoned that "the criterion should be whether the disclosure [was] sufficient to enable one skilled in the art to reduce the disclosed invention to practice. In other words, the disclosure must [have been such as would] give possession of the invention to the person of ordinary skill." While actual or constructive reduction to practice would sufficiently disclose the invention, some other form of disclosure [in that case, an unpublished document] containing "a description of the invention fully commensurate with" a patent application could, too. Thus, as long as the disclosure was enabling, it "need not be of an invention reduced to practice, either actually or constructively." *Id.*, 345 F.2d at 855.

The *Borst* decision did not provide much guidance with regard to the second requirement--that the invention have been accessible to the public. Since "publications" constitute a separate category of prior art, presumably public disclosures that fall short of "publication" can qualify to make an invention "known" within the meaning of subsection (a). In Oak Industries, Inc. v. Zenith Electronics Corp., 726 F.Supp. 1525 (N.D.Ill.1989), the earlier inventor had demonstrated the invention to some visiting engineers from out of town. The court reasoned that by demonstrating or describing the invention to the visitors (who were skilled in the relevant art, and for purposes of the summary judgment motion, were presumed to have owed no duty of confidentiality), the first inventor made the invention available to the public. This was because the recipients of the disclosure, who were skilled in the art, were in a position to further disseminate the information, or use it to the public's benefit in their own work.

*b) The invention was used by others in this country prior to the applicant's invention.* Prior use of an invention, by its nature, requires that the invention have been actually reduced to practice. In addition, the prior use of the invention must have been accessible to the public. Connecticut Valley Enterprises, Inc. v. United States, 348 F.2d 949, 952 (Ct.Cl.1965). However, in this context, the "accessibility" requirement entails little more than an absence of affirmative steps to conceal. If the prior invention was used in the manner for which it was intended, the prior user need not have taken any affirmative steps to make the invention known widely to the public or to those skilled in the art. Moreover, the prior use need not have led to public understanding of the invention. Gillman v. Stern, 114 F.2d 28 (2d Cir.1940), *cert. denied*, 311 U.S. 718 (1941).

*c) The invention was patented in this or a foreign country before the applicant's invention.* Patents generally become part of the prior art for purposes of anticipation on the date they become effective, provided that their contents are at least minimally accessible to the public. In order to anticipate, the patent must fully describe the later invention. Why is it necessary to provide that prior patents will anticipate a U.S. invention? Won't patents also constitute "printed publications?" Note that while most U.S. patent applications are published 18 months after they are filed, and issued patents are also published (in both cases creating a “printed publication”), that may not be true in the case of foreign patents.

*d) The invention was described in a printed publication in this or a foreign country before the applicant's invention.* A "printed publication" must describe the invention sufficiently to enable a person having ordinary skill in the art to make or practice the invention without undue experimentation.

> The statutory phrase "printed publication" has been interpreted to give effect to ongoing advances in the technologies of data storage, retrieval, and dissemination. Because there are many ways in which a reference may be disseminated to the interested public, "public accessibility" has been called the touchstone in determining whether a reference constitutes a "printed publication" * * *. [It must appear that] the reference was sufficiently accessible, at least to the public interested in the art, so that such a one by examining the reference could make the claimed invention without further research or experimentation.

*In re* Hall, 781 F.2d 897, 898-99 (Fed.Cir.1986).

The range of references that may constitute a printed publication is quite wide: microfilm, photographs, and slides have all been found sufficient. It seems clear, however, that the information must be "fixed" or made tangible. Presumably, if a sales person at a trade show orally described a new invention to customers, this would not create a printed publication for purposes of § 102, no matter how detailed and precise the description.

When will a tangible reference be sufficiently accessible to the public to constitute a printed publication? In *In re* Wyer, 655 F.2d 221 (C.C.P.A. 1981), microfilm copies of a patent application were made available upon request in the Australian Patent Office and in its five sub-offices, and means were available in these locations for visitors to make their own copies. The Court of Customs and Patent Appeals found this sufficient to constitute a printed publication. In *Hall*, *supra*, the Federal Circuit found that a single graduate thesis in one German university library was sufficiently accessible, since it was indexed in a special dissertations catalog which was part of the general users' catalog, and was freely available to students, faculty and the general public. By contrast, in *In re* Cronyn, 890 F.2d 1158 (Fed.Cir.1989), the Federal Circuit found that a student thesis at an American college did not constitute a printed publication. In that case, undergraduate theses were described on individual index cards, which were filed alphabetically under the authors' names and kept in a shoe box in the chemistry department library. The court noted that these theses were not sufficiently accessible to the public since they were not cataloged or indexed in a meaningful way.

In Massachusetts Institute of Technology v. AB Fortia, 774 F.2d 1104 (Fed.Cir.1985), a paper was presented orally at a conference attended by 50 to 500 persons skilled in the subject matter. A copy of the paper was provided to the head of the conference and copies were distributed on request, without any restrictions, to as many as six persons. The court found that the paper constituted a printed publication. Compare Northern Telecom, Inc. v. Datapoint Corp., 908 F.2d 931 (Fed.Cir.), *cert. denied*, 498 U.S. 920 (1990), in which the Federal Circuit declined to find a printed publication. In that case, four reports were distributed to approximately fifty persons or organizations involved in a complex military project. While the reports were not under security classification, some or all of the reports contained the legend "Reproduction or further dissemination is not authorized ... not for public release." The reports were also housed in the library of a private corporation, with library access restricted to authorized persons. The court reasoned that there was no clear and convincing evidence that an interested person could have had access to the documents through the exercise of reasonable diligence.

In *In re* Klopfenstein, 380 F.3d 1345 (Fed. Cir. 2004), the inventors of a method of preparing foods containing extruded soy cotyledon fiber prepared a slide presentation that fully disclosed their invention. They printed the fourteen slides and pasted them on to poster boards and displayed the boards continuously for two and a half days at a meeting of the American Association of Cereal Chemists. Shortly thereafter they put the same slide presentation on display for part of a day at an Agriculture Experiment Station at a university. The inventors did not provide a disclaimer or notice to the intended audience prohibiting note-taking or copying of the presentation. However, they did not disseminate any copies of the presentation.

The Court of Appeals for the Federal Circuit found that the display constituted a printed publication, rejecting arguments that a disclosure must be either disseminated, indexed at a library, or cataloged in a database to qualify. The court reiterated that public accessibility is the key to finding a printed publication. It reasoned that in the absence of distribution or indexing, several factors should be considered to determine whether the reference was sufficiently publicly accessible: 1) the length of time the display was exhibited; 2) the expertise of the target audience; 3) the existence (or lack thereof) of reasonable expectations that the displayed material would not be copied; and 4) the simplicity or ease with which the displayed material could have been copied. *Id.*, 380 F.3d at 1350. Here, the poster boards had been displayed for three days to a audience comprised of persons with ordinary skill in the art of cereal chemistry. There were no facts to suggest that the inventors could expect the audience not to copy the information. Moreover, it would be relatively simple to copy the information from the boards, since the key information was concentrated on only a few of the boards, and each of these boards consisted of only three bulleted items of two concise sentences or less. Given this liberal opportunity for the audience of persons skilled in the art to copy, the court reasoned that it was appropriate to consider the display a printed publication.

3. *Section 102(e).* In Alexander Milburn Co. v. Davis-Bournonville Co., 270 U.S. 390, 46 S.Ct. 324, 70 L.Ed. 651 (1926), the plaintiff obtained a patent for an improvement in a welding and cutting apparatus, and later sued the defendant for infringement. The defendant challenged the validity of the plaintiff's patent, alleging that plaintiff's inventor, Whitford, was not the first inventor. Whitford's alleged invention date was March 4, 1911--the date he filed his patent application. Plaintiff's patent issued on June 4, 1912. Evidence indicated that Clifford applied for a patent on January 31, 1911, which issued on February 6, 1912. Clifford's application gave a complete and adequate description of the improvement patented to Whitford, but did not claim it. The Supreme Court found that the disclosure in Clifford's application (which was retained in confidence by the PTO while the Clifford application pended) invalidated plaintiff's patent:

> We understand the Circuit Court of Appeals to admit that if Whitford had not applied for his patent until after the issue to Clifford, the disclosure by the latter would have had

> the same effect as the publication of the same words in a periodical, although not made the basis of a claim. The invention is made public property as much in the one case as in the other. But if this be true, as we think that it is, it seems to us that a sound distinction cannot be taken between that case and a patent applied for before but not granted until after a second patent is sought. The delays of the Patent Office ought not to cut down the effect of what has been done. The description shows that Whitford was not the first inventor. Clifford had done all that he could do to make his description public. He had taken steps that would make it public as soon as the Patent Office did its work, although, of course, amendments might be required of him before the end could be reached. We see no reason in the words or policy of the law for allowing Whitford to profit by the delay and make himself out to be the first inventor when he was not so in fact, when Clifford had shown knowledge inconsistent with the allowance of Whitford's claim, and when otherwise the publication of his patent would abandon the thing described to the public unless it already was old.

*Id.*, 270 U.S. at 401-02. In its subsequent revision of the patent laws, Congress codified the holding in *Milburn* by adopting 35 U.S.C. §102(e), which provides that a person shall be entitled to a patent unless the invention was described in "a patent granted on an application for patent by another filed in the United States before the invention by the applicant * * * ". Note that if the earlier-filed application is granted, the disclosures contained in the patent become a part of the prior art *as of the time the application was filed*, rather than at the time the patent issues and is published. See Hazeltine Research, Inc. v. Brenner, 382 U.S. 252, 86 S.Ct. 335, 15 L.Ed.2d 304 (1965).

At the time the *Milburn* case was decided, and for many years thereafter, the PTO kept patent applications in confidence until the patent issued, at which point the patent, with its claims and enabling disclosure, was published. In the Intellectual Property and Communications Omnibus Reform Act of 1999, Congress amended Patent Act § 122 to provide that the PTO should publish most patent applications 18 months after their filing date. It simultaneously amended § 102(e) to provide that a person will not be entitled to a patent if the invention was described in "an application for patent, published under section 122(b), by another filed in the United States before the invention by the applicant for patent * * *." Pub. L. No. 106-113, ' 4505, 113 Stat. at 1537-557.[4] An accompanying section-by-section analysis explained:

> Section 4505 amends section 102(e) of the Patent Act to treat an application published by the USPTO in the same fashion as a patent granted by the USPTO. Accordingly, a published application is given prior art effect as of its earliest effective U.S. filing date against any subsequently filed U.S. applications.

145 Cong. Rec. S14719 (daily ed. Nov. 17, 1999) (included in the record at the request of Sen. Lott). Disclosures in pending patent applications that are later granted or published are sometimes referred to as "secret prior art," because at the time that the later inventor invented, it might have been impossible for her to learn of the disclosures.

4. *Section 102(g).* Section 102(g) denies a patent for an invention if, before the applicant's invention date, "the invention was made in this country by another inventor who had not abandoned, suppressed or concealed it." 35 U.S.C. § 102(g).[5] What is the policy behind permitting a later inventor to obtain a patent if the earlier inventor has abandoned, suppressed or concealed the invention?

---

[4]Section 102(e) also provides that international patent applications filed pursuant to the Patent Cooperation Treaty ("PCT") should be treated as applications filed in the U.S., but only if they designate the U.S. and are published under PCT Art. 21(2) in English. For more information about the PCT, see pages 244-46, *infra.*

[5] An earlier invention abroad can also serve as a basis for rejecting an application, if the earlier foreign inventor establishes, "during the course of an interference conducted under section 135 or section 291," her earlier invention date and a lack of abandonment, suppression or concealment. 35 U.S.C. § 102(g)(1).

When will an abandonment, suppression or concealment be found? The Court of Appeals for the Federal Circuit addressed this issue in Checkpoint Systems, Inc. v. U.S. International Trade Commission, 54 F.3d 756 (Fed. Cir. 1995):

> * * * A principal purpose of § 102(g) is to ensure that a patent is awarded to a first inventor. However, it also encourages prompt public disclosure of an invention by penalizing the unexcused delay or failure of a first inventor to share the "benefit of the knowledge of [the] invention" with the public after the invention has been completed.
>
> When determining whether an inventor has abandoned, suppressed, or concealed an invention, a period of delay between completion of the invention and subsequent public disclosure may or may not be of legal consequence. The delay may be inconsequential if, for example, it is reasonable in length or excused by activities of the inventor. Furthermore, there is no particular length of delay that is per se unreasonable. Rather, a determination of abandonment, suppression, or concealment has "consistently been based on equitable principles and public policy as applied to the facts of each case." A court must determine whether, under the facts before it, any delay was reasonable or excused as a matter of law.
>
> One way a prior inventor may avoid the disqualifying effect of § 102(g) is by promptly filing a patent application claiming the invention. In the usual context of an interference proceeding, each inventor involved in the proceeding will have filed a patent application, one of which may have matured into a patent. However, § 102(g) is applicable in other contexts as well, such as when it is asserted as a basis for invalidating a patent in defense to an infringement suit. In such a case, a first inventor may seek to avoid a determination of abandonment by showing that he or she marketed or sold a commercial embodiment of the invention or described the invention in a publicly disseminated document. See *Palmer v. Dudzik*, 481 F.2d 1377, 1387(CCPA 1973) (to negate a finding of

> suppression or concealment, the public must have gained knowledge of the invention which will insure its preservation in the public domain). If the prior inventor's activities following completion of the invention do not evidence abandonment, suppression, or concealment, § 102(g) will bar a later inventor from obtaining a patent. In cases in which an invention is disclosed to the public by commercialization, courts have excused delay upon proof that the first inventor engaged in reasonable efforts to bring the invention to market. See, e.g., *Engelhard Corp. v. M.C. Canfield Sons*, 13 USPQ2d 1561, 1564-65 (D.N.J.1989) ("[T]he company's delay was within the realm of 'reasonable business practices.' "); *Refac Elecs. Corp. v. R.H. Macy & Co.*, 9 USPQ2d 1497, 1506 (D.N.J.1988) ("The pivotal issue ... is whether the 'nature and tempo' of [the] activities between the initial invention/reduction-to-practice and ultimate market distribution are in accord with reasonable business practices...."), aff'd mem., 871 F.2d 1097 (Fed.Cir.1989). * * *

*Id.* 54 F.3d at 761-62. Assuming that the earlier inventor is engaging in "reasonable business practices" while gearing up to commercialize the invention, should it matter if she keeps it secret prior to its market release?

Suppose that the first inventor abandons, suppresses or conceals his invention, but later resumes activity and files a patent application. Will § 102(g) deprive him of a patent if no second inventor has appeared on the scene and filed an application? What if a second inventor files an application, but only after the first inventor has resumed? Consider Paulik v. Rizkalla, 760 F.2d 1270 (Fed.Cir.1985).

In *Paulik*, Paulik, an employee of the Monsanto Company, reduced his invention to practice in November, 1970, and again in April, 1971. Paulik immediately sent information about the invention to the Patent Department of his assignee, the Monsanto Company. While the Patent Department kept the project on active status, it assigned it a lower priority than other pending projects. Despite prodding from Paulik, the Patent Department only began work toward filing a patent application in January or February of 1975. On March 10, 1975, Rizkalla filed an application for patent for the same invention. On June 30, 1975, Monsanto's Patent Department filed its application for the Paulik invention. In the subsequent interference proceeding, Rizkalla relied on his filing date as his date of invention. The PTO Board of Patent Interferences held that Paulik's four-year delay from reduction to practice to filing was *prima facie* suppression or concealment, and awarded priority to Rizkalla. The Federal Circuit vacated and remanded.

The court held that Paulik was entitled to demonstrate that he (through his assignee) had renewed activity on the invention and had proceeded diligently to file his patent application from a date prior to Rizkalla's invention date. Upon making this proof, he could rely on his date of renewed activity as his date of invention for purposes of the priority determination. While Paulik's four years of inactivity would deprive him of the benefit of his original date of invention, his date of renewed activity, which predated Rizkalla's invention, would entitle him to priority and a patent. The court reasoned:

> The reason for the patent system is to encourage innovation and its fruits: new jobs and new industries, new consumer goods and trade benefits. We must keep this purpose in plain view as we consider the consequences of interpretations of the patent law such as in the Board's decision.
>
> A foreseeable consequence of the Board's ruling is to discourage inventors and their supporters from working on projects that had been "too long" set aside, because of the impossibility of relying, in a priority contest, on either their original work or their renewed work. This curious result is neither fair nor in the public interest. We do not see that the public interest is served by placing so severe a sanction on failure to file premature patent applications on immature inventions of unknown value. In reversing the Board's decision we do not hold that such inventions are necessarily entitled to the benefits of their earliest dates in a priority contest; we hold only that they are not barred from entitlement to their dates of renewed activity.

*Id.*, 760 F.2d at 1276.

[*Problem*]- Exam

1. Allen and Brown, U.S. university research professors, conceived of a new kind of widget and reduced it to actual practice in November, 2006. They made no attempt to license, manufacture or sell the widget, or to put their prototype to use. They also decided not to apply for a patent. They did not tell others about the invention, but went to work right away to write a paper that described it, and the scientific principles underlying it, working diligently on the paper until it was completed in February, 2008. They then submitted the paper to a scientific journal for publication, and the journal published it in September, 2008.

In December, 2006, Chen, a U.S. manufacturer of widgets, invented a widget that had all the same elements as Allen and Brown's. At that time, Chen decided not to file for a patent, and she also decided not to manufacture the widget for sale right away. She decided to postpone manufacture because she already had plans to renovate her factory in 2010, and she felt that it would be more cost efficient to undertake the manufacture after the renovations were complete. Meanwhile, Chen kept the widget secret, but engaged in no further work in connection with it.

In July, 2007, Davis invented a widget that had all the same elements as Allen and Brown's. He made his invention in South Africa, and during the next year, manufactured and sold 200 of the widgets in that country. Davis did not apply for a patent.

In January, 2008, Effinger invented a widget with the same elements as Allen and Brown's. In February, 2008, Chen changed her mind about patenting her widget, and applied for a patent. In March, 2008, Effinger filed a patent application, too.

Assume that the widget is "useful" and that in 2006, it was both novel and non-obvious. Evaluate Chen's and Effinger's right to a patent under pre-AIA Patent Act § 102.

### b. The Pre-America Invents Act Statutory Bar Provisions

## Moleculon Research Corp. v. CBS, Inc.

United States Court of Appeals, Federal Circuit, 1986.
793 F.2d 1261, *cert. denied*, 479 U.S. 1030 (1987).

Baldwin, Circuit Judge.

* * *

A puzzle enthusiast since childhood, Nichols, in the summer of 1957, conceived of a three-dimensional puzzle capable of rotational movement. He envisioned an assembly of eight cubes attached in a 2 x 2 x 2 arrangement, with each of the six faces of the composite cube distinguished by a different color and the individual cubes being capable of rotation in sets of four around one of three mutually perpendicular axes.

During the period 1957-1962, while doing graduate work in organic chemistry, Nichols constructed several paper models of his puzzle, making cubes of heavy file-card type paper and affixing small magnets to the inside of the cubes. Although these models confirmed the feasibility of Nichols' conception, they lacked durability. A few close friends, including two roommates and a colleague in the chemistry department, had occasion to see one of these paper models in Nichols' room and Nichols explained its operation to at least one of them.

In 1962, Nichols accepted employment as a research scientist at Moleculon. In 1968, Nichols constructed a working wood block prototype of his puzzle which he usually kept at home but on occasion brought into his office. In January 1969, Dr. Obermayer, the president of Moleculon, entered Nichols' office and happened to see the model sitting on his desk. Obermayer expressed immediate interest in the puzzle and Nichols explained its workings. Obermayer asked whether

Nichols intended to commercialize the puzzle. When Nichols said no, Obermayer suggested that Moleculon try to do so. In March 1969, Nichols assigned all his rights in the puzzle invention to Moleculon in return for a share of any proceeds of commercialization. On March 7, 1969, Moleculon sent Parker Brothers an actual model and a description of the cube puzzle. In the next three years, Moleculon contacted between fifty and sixty toy and game manufacturers, including Ideal. Ideal responded to the effect that it did not currently have an interest in marketing the puzzle. Moleculon itself did not succeed in marketing the Nichols cube.

On March 3, 1970, Nichols filed on behalf of Moleculon a patent application covering his invention. The '201 patent issued on April 11, 1972.

[In this suit, Moleculon alleges that the well-known Rubik's Cube puzzle infringes the '201 patent.]

*1. § 102(b) on sale and public use bars*

CBS argues that the subject matter of the '201 patent was in "public use" and "on sale" by Nichols, prior to the March 3, 1969 critical date (i.e., one year prior to filing of the patent application), thus rendering the patent invalid under section 102(b).

*(a) Public Use*

CBS labels as public use Nichols' displaying of the models to other persons (such as his colleagues at school) without any mention of secrecy. CBS ascribes only commercial purpose and intent to Obermayer's use of the wood model and argues that a conclusion of barring public use under §102(b) is compelled. We disagree.

This is what the district court had to say:

> The essence of "public use" is the free and unrestricted giving over of an invention to a member of the public or the public in general. What I see here, by contrast, is the inventor's private use of his own invention for his own enjoyment. "Private use of one's own invention is permissible."

> While it is true that Nichols explained his puzzle to a few close colleagues who inquired about it and allowed Obermayer to in fact use it, the personal relationships and other surrounding circumstances were such that Nichols at all times retained control over its use as well as over the distribution of information concerning it. He never used the puzzle or permitted it used in a place or at a time when he did not have a legitimate expectation of privacy and of confidentiality. In these respects, I consider the exposure to Obermayer in Nichols' office no different than the exposure of Nichols' close friends in his home.
>
> Here also the relationship between the participants in the alleged uses evidences a retention of control by Nichols. None of those participants had any basis for inferring that the puzzle was being given over by Nichols for their free and unrestricted use. Holding the public use bar inapplicable in these circumstances will not remove anything from the public domain. Moreover, there is absolutely no evidence in this case of commercially motivated activity by Nichols during the relevant period. [Accordingly, the underlying policy against extending the effective term of exclusivity is not offended by a finding that the Nichols invention was not in public use.]

CBS correctly recognizes that the district court's conclusion on public use under § 102(b) is subject to review as a question of law while the facts underlying the conclusion on public use are subject to the clearly erroneous standard of review.

CBS urges that the decision in *Egbert v. Lippmann*, 104 U.S. 333, 26 L.Ed. 755 (1881), compels a conclusion of public use in the present case. In *Egbert*, the claimed invention was drawn to improved corset-springs, also called corset-steels. In 1855, the inventor made and presented to his lady friend a pair of corset-steels which embodied the invention. She wore the steels for a long time. The inventor made and gave her another pair three years later which she also wore a long time. On several occasions, when the corset itself wore out, the steels were removed and placed into a new corset. In 1866, an application for patent was filed. It was on those facts that the Court observed that: "If an inventor, having made his device, gives or sells it to another, to be used by the donee or vendee, without limitation or restriction, or injunction of secrecy, and it is so used, such use is public, even though the use and knowledge of the use may be confined to one person."

The district court distinguished *Egbert* because here Nichols had not given over the invention for free and unrestricted use by another person. Based on the personal relationships and surrounding circumstances, the court found that Nichols at all times retained control over the puzzle's use and the distribution of information concerning it. The court characterized Nichols' use as private and for his own enjoyment. We see neither legal error in the analysis nor clear error in the findings.

As for Obermayer's brief use of the puzzle, the court found that Nichols retained control even though he and Obermayer had not entered into any express confidentiality agreement. The court held, and we agree, that the presence or absence of such an agreement is not determinative of the public use issue. It is one factor to be considered in assessing all the evidence. There can be no question that the court looked at the totality of evidence, and evaluated that evidence in view of time, place, and circumstances.

With regard to the question of control, CBS complains that "[t]he record is devoid of any testimony from the friends, associates and fellow workers who saw Nichols' cube and to whom its operation was explained." The simple answer is that CBS had the burden at trial to prove public use with facts supported by clear and convincing evidence. We think the district court's characterization of the evidence of record is entirely apt and we see no ground for reversal. Moreover, we agree with the district court that its conclusion on public use is consistent with the policies underlying the bar.

CBS further argues in connection with public use that the district court erred when it found no evidence of commercially motivated activity by Nichols prior to the critical date.[3] Although CBS attempts to paint a picture of commercialization from the discussions between Obermayer and Nichols, we see only the brush strokes of speculation. The record lacks hard evidence. Discussion between employer and employee does not by itself convert an employee's private pursuit into commercial enterprise with the employer. CBS also makes much of a February 6, 1969 phone call by Obermayer to Parker Brothers to see if the latter was interested in receiving a submission of a puzzle idea from an outside inventor. Nothing concerning the nature or workings of Nichols' puzzle was disclosed. Obermayer simply inquired whether and how an outsider could submit a puzzle for Parker Brothers' consideration. We agree with the district court that those facts do not show commercialization. Thus this case differs from other cases where commercial activity was said to violate the policies of section 102(b).

*(b) On Sale*

CBS argues that the claimed invention was on sale within the meaning of 35 U.S.C. § 102(b) because Nichols orally agreed prior to the critical date (e.g., during a January 1969 conversation between Nichols and Obermayer) to assign "all his rights in the puzzle invention" to Moleculon. According to CBS, Nichols not only assigned the right to apply for a patent on the invention but also conveyed title in his single wooden model.

Although the formal written assignment occurred after the critical date, the district court held that even if there were an earlier oral agreement, an assignment or sale of the rights in the invention and potential patent rights is not a sale of "the invention" within the meaning of section 102(b). We agree. The few cases we have found on this issue have uniformly held that such a sale of patent rights does not come within the section 102(b) bar. Such a result comports with the policies underlying the on sale bar, and with the business realities

---

[3]In some instances, commercially motivated activities may implicate both the public use and the on sale bars.

ordinarily surrounding a corporation's prosecution of patent applications for inventors.

As for CBS' contention that Nichols sold or agreed to sell the wood model of the puzzle, we quote the district court's relevant findings:

> There is no indication in the subsequent written instrument that the parties contemplated the sale or transfer to Moleculon of the single physical embodiment of the puzzle then in existence. Nor is there any other evidence in the record to that effect.

CBS has shown nothing approaching clear error concerning those findings.

Accordingly, we sustain the district court's determination that the claims are not invalid under section 102(b).
* * *

## Pfaff v. Wells Electronics, Inc.

United States Supreme Court, 1998.
525 U.S. 55, 119 S.Ct. 304, 142 L.Ed.2d 261.

Justice Stevens delivered the opinion of the [unanimous] Court.

Section 102(b) of the Patent Act of 1952 provides that no person is entitled to patent an "invention" that has been "on sale" more than one year before filing a patent application.[1] We granted certiorari

---

[1]"A person shall be entitled to a patent unless--

....

"(b) the invention was patented or described in a printed publication in this or a foreign country or in public use or on sale in this country, more than one year prior to the date of the application for patent in the United States, or...."

35 U.S.C. § 102.

to determine whether the commercial marketing of a newly invented product may mark the beginning of the 1-year period even though the invention has not yet been reduced to practice.[2]

I

On April 19, 1982, petitioner, Wayne Pfaff, filed an application for a patent on a computer chip socket. Therefore, April 19, 1981, constitutes the critical date for purposes of the on-sale bar of 35 U.S.C. § 102(b); if the 1-year period began to run before that date, Pfaff lost his right to patent his invention.

Pfaff commenced work on the socket in November 1980, when representatives of Texas Instruments asked him to develop a new device for mounting and removing semiconductor chip carriers. In response to this request, he prepared detailed engineering drawings that described the design, the dimensions, and the materials to be used in making the socket. Pfaff sent those drawings to a manufacturer in February or March 1981.

Prior to March 17, 1981, Pfaff showed a sketch of his concept to representatives of Texas Instruments. On April 8, 1981, they provided Pfaff with a written confirmation of a previously placed oral purchase order for 30,100 of his new sockets for a total price of $91,155. In accord with his normal practice, Pfaff did not make and test a prototype of the new device before offering to sell it in commercial quantities.

The manufacturer took several months to develop the customized tooling necessary to produce the device, and Pfaff did not

---

[2] "A process is reduced to practice when it is successfully performed. A machine is reduced to practice when it is assembled adjusted and used. A manufacture is reduced to practice when it is completely manufactured. A composition of matter is reduced to practice when it is completely composed." *Corona Cord Tire Co. v. Dovan Chemical Corp.*, 276 U.S. 358, 383, 48 S.Ct. 380, 72 L.Ed. 610 (1928).

fill the order until July 1981. The evidence therefore indicates that Pfaff first reduced his invention to practice in the summer of 1981. The socket achieved substantial commercial success before Patent No. 4,491,377 (the '377 patent) issued to Pfaff on January 1, 1985. After the patent issued, petitioner brought an infringement action against respondent, Wells Electronics, Inc., the manufacturer of a competing socket. [The district court found some of the claims valid and infringed. It rejected Wells' § 102(b) defense, finding that the one-year statutory period did not begin to run until petitioner reduced his invention to practice.]

The Court of Appeals reversed, finding all six claims invalid. Four of the claims (1, 6, 7, and 10) described the socket that Pfaff had sold to Texas Instruments prior to April 8, 1981. Because that device had been offered for sale on a commercial basis more than one year before the patent application was filed on April 19, 1982, the court concluded that those claims were invalid under § 102(b). That conclusion rested on the court's view that as long as the invention was "substantially complete at the time of sale," the 1-year period began to run, even though the invention had not yet been reduced to practice. * * *

Because other courts have held or assumed that an invention cannot be "on sale" within the meaning of § 102(b) unless and until it has been reduced to practice, and because the text of § 102(b) makes no reference to "substantial completion" of an invention, we granted certiorari.

II

The primary meaning of the word "invention" in the Patent Act unquestionably refers to the inventor's conception rather than to a physical embodiment of that idea. The statute does not contain any express requirement that an invention must be reduced to practice before it can be patented. Neither the statutory definition of the term in § 100[8] nor the basic conditions for obtaining a patent set forth in §

---

[8]Title 35 § 100, "Definitions," states,

"When used in this title unless the context otherwise indicates--

101[9] make any mention of "reduction to practice." The statute's only specific reference to that term is found in § 102(g), which sets forth the standard for resolving priority contests between two competing claimants to a patent. That subsection provides:

> "In determining priority of invention there shall be considered not only the respective dates of conception and reduction to practice of the invention, but also the reasonable diligence of one who was first to conceive and last to reduce to practice, from a time prior to conception by the other."

Thus, assuming diligence on the part of the applicant, it is normally the first inventor to conceive, rather than the first to reduce to practice, who establishes the right to the patent.

It is well settled that an invention may be patented before it is reduced to practice. In 1888, this Court upheld a patent issued to Alexander Graham Bell even though he had filed his application before constructing a working telephone. Chief Justice Waite's reasoning in that case merits quoting at length:

> "It is quite true that when Bell applied for his patent he had never actually transmitted telegraphically spoken words so that they could be distinctly heard and understood at the receiving end of his line, but in his specification he did describe accurately and with admirable clearness his process, that is to say, the exact electrical condition that must be created to accomplish his purpose, and he also described, with sufficient

---

"(a) The term 'invention' means invention or discovery...."

[9]Section 101, "Inventions patentable," provides,

"Whoever invents or discovers any new and useful process, machine, manufacture, or composition of matter, or any new and useful improvement thereof, may obtain a patent therefor, subject to the conditions and requirements of this title."

> precision to enable one of ordinary skill in such matters to make it, a form of apparatus which, if used in the way pointed out, would produce the required effect, receive the words, and carry them to and deliver them at the appointed place. The particular instrument which he had, and which he used in his experiments, did not, under the circumstances in which it was tried, reproduce the words spoken, so that they could be clearly understood, but the proof is abundant and of the most convincing character, that other instruments, carefully constructed and made exactly in accordance with the specification, without any additions whatever, have operated and will operate successfully. A good mechanic of proper skill in matters of the kind can take the patent and, by following the specification strictly, can, without more, construct an apparatus which, when used in the way pointed out, will do all that it is claimed the method or process will do....
>
> "The law does not require that a discoverer or inventor, in order to get a patent for a process, must have succeeded in bringing his art to the highest degree of perfection. It is enough if he describes his method with sufficient clearness and precision to enable those skilled in the matter to understand what the process is, and if he points out some practicable way of putting it into operation."

*The Telephone Cases*, 126 U.S. 1, 536, 8 S.Ct. 778, 31 L.Ed. 863 (1888).[10]

When we apply the reasoning of The Telephone Cases to the facts of the case before us today, it is evident that Pfaff could have

---

[10] This Court has also held a patent invalid because the invention had previously been disclosed in a prior patent application, although that application did not claim the invention and the first invention apparently had not been reduced to practice. *Alexander Milburn Co. v. Davis-Bournonville Co.*, 270 U.S. 390, 401-402, 46 S.Ct. 324, 70 L.Ed. 651 (1926).

obtained a patent on his novel socket when he accepted the purchase order from Texas Instruments for 30,100 units. At that time he provided the manufacturer with a description and drawings that had "sufficient clearness and precision to enable those skilled in the matter" to produce the device. The parties agree that the sockets manufactured to fill that order embody Pfaff's conception as set forth in claims 1, 6, 7, and 10 of the '377 patent. We can find no basis in the text of § 102(b) or in the facts of this case for concluding that Pfaff's invention was not "on sale" within the meaning of the statute until after it had been reduced to practice.

III

Pfaff nevertheless argues that longstanding precedent, buttressed by the strong interest in providing inventors with a clear standard identifying the onset of the 1-year period, justifies a special interpretation of the word "invention" as used in § 102(b). We are persuaded that this nontextual argument should be rejected.

As we have often explained, most recently in *Bonito Boats, Inc. v. Thunder Craft Boats, Inc.*, 489 U.S. 141, 151, 109 S.Ct. 971, 103 L.Ed.2d 118 (1989), the patent system represents a carefully crafted bargain that encourages both the creation and the public disclosure of new and useful advances in technology, in return for an exclusive monopoly for a limited period of time. The balance between the interest in motivating innovation and enlightenment by rewarding invention with patent protection on the one hand, and the interest in avoiding monopolies that unnecessarily stifle competition on the other, has been a feature of the federal patent laws since their inception. As this Court explained in 1871:

> "Letters patent are not to be regarded as monopolies ... but as public franchises granted to the inventors of new and useful improvements for the purpose of securing to them, as such inventors, for the limited term therein mentioned, the exclusive right and liberty to make and use and vend to others to be used their own inventions, as tending to promote the progress of science and the useful arts, and as a matter of compensation to the inventors for their labor, toil, and expense in making the inventions, and reducing the same to practice for the public

> benefit, as contemplated by the Constitution and sanctioned by the laws of Congress."

*Seymour v. Osborne*, 11 Wall. 516, 533-534.

Consistent with these ends, §102 of the Patent Act serves as a limiting provision, both excluding ideas that are in the public domain from patent protection and confining the duration of the monopoly to the statutory term.

We originally held that an inventor loses his right to a patent if he puts his invention into public use before filing a patent application. "His voluntary act or acquiescence in the public sale and use is an abandonment of his right" *Pennock v. Dialogue*, 2 Pet. 1, 24, 7 L.Ed. 327 (1829) (Story, J.). A similar reluctance to allow an inventor to remove existing knowledge from public use undergirds the on-sale bar.

Nevertheless, an inventor who seeks to perfect his discovery may conduct extensive testing without losing his right to obtain a patent for his invention--even if such testing occurs in the public eye. The law has long recognized the distinction between inventions put to experimental use and products sold commercially. In 1878, we explained why patentability may turn on an inventor's use of his product.

> "It is sometimes said that an inventor acquires an undue advantage over the public by delaying to take out a patent, inasmuch as he thereby preserves the monopoly to himself for a longer period than is allowed by the policy of the law; but this cannot be said with justice when the delay is occasioned by a bona fide effort to bring his invention to perfection, or to ascertain whether it will answer the purpose intended. His monopoly only continues for the allotted period, in any event; and it is the interest of the public, as well as himself, that the invention should be perfect and properly tested, before a patent is granted for it. Any attempt to use it for a profit, and not by way of experiment, for a longer period than two years before the application, would deprive the inventor of his right to a patent."

*Elizabeth v. American Nicholson Pavement Co.*, 97 U.S. 126, 137, 24 L.Ed. 1000 (1877).

The patent laws therefore seek both to protect the public's right to retain knowledge already in the public domain and the inventor's right to control whether and when he may patent his invention. The Patent Act of 1836, 5 Stat. 117, was the first statute that expressly included an on-sale bar to the issuance of a patent. Like the earlier holding in Pennock, that provision precluded patentability if the invention had been placed on sale at any time before the patent application was filed. In 1839, Congress ameliorated that requirement by enacting a 2-year grace period in which the inventor could file an application. 5 Stat. 353.

In *Andrews v. Hovey*, 123 U.S. 267, 274, 8 S.Ct. 101, 31 L.Ed. 160 (1887), we noted that the purpose of that amendment was "to fix a period of limitation which should be certain"; it required the inventor to make sure that a patent application was filed "within two years from the completion of his invention," *ibid.* In 1939, Congress reduced the grace period from two years to one year. 53 Stat. 1212.

Petitioner correctly argues that these provisions identify an interest in providing inventors with a definite standard for determining when a patent application must be filed. A rule that makes the timeliness of an application depend on the date when an invention is "substantially complete" seriously undermines the interest in certainty.[11] Moreover, such a rule finds no support in the text of the

---

[11]The Federal Circuit has developed a multifactor, "totality of the circumstances" test to determine the trigger for the on-sale bar. See, e.g., *Micro Chemical, Inc. v. Great Plains Chemical Co.*, 103 F.3d 1538, 1544 (C.A.Fed.1997) (stating that, in determining whether an invention is on sale for purposes of 102(b), " 'all of the circumstances surrounding the sale or offer to sell, including the stage of development of the invention and the nature of the invention, must be considered and weighed against the policies underlying section 102(b)' "); *see also UMC Electronics Co. v. United States,* 816 F.2d 647, 656 (1987) (stating the on-sale bar "does not lend itself to formulation into

statute. Thus, petitioner's argument calls into question the standard applied by the Court of Appeals, but it does not persuade us that it is necessary to engraft a reduction to practice element into the meaning of the term "invention" as used in §102(b).

The word "invention" must refer to a concept that is complete, rather than merely one that is "substantially complete." It is true that reduction to practice ordinarily provides the best evidence that an invention is complete. But just because reduction to practice is sufficient evidence of completion, it does not follow that proof of reduction to practice is necessary in every case. Indeed, both the facts of the *Telephone Cases* and the facts of this case demonstrate that one can prove that an invention is complete and ready for patenting before it has actually been reduced to practice.

We conclude, therefore, that the on-sale bar applies when two conditions are satisfied before the critical date. First, the product must be the subject of a commercial offer for sale. An inventor can both understand and control the timing of the first commercial marketing of his invention. The experimental use doctrine, for example, has not generated concerns about indefiniteness, and we perceive no reason why unmanageable uncertainty should attend a rule that measures the application of the on-sale bar of §102(b) against the date when an invention that is ready for patenting is first marketed commercially. In this case the acceptance of the purchase order prior to April 8, 1981, makes it clear that such an offer had been made, and there is no question that the sale was commercial rather than experimental in character.

Second, the invention must be ready for patenting. That condition may be satisfied in at least two ways: by proof of reduction to practice before the critical date; or by proof that prior to the critical date the inventor had prepared drawings or other descriptions of the invention that were sufficiently specific to enable a person skilled in

---

a set of precise requirements"). As the Federal Circuit itself has noted, this test "has been criticized as unnecessarily vague."

the art to practice the invention. In this case the second condition of the on-sale bar is satisfied because the drawings Pfaff sent to the manufacturer before the critical date fully disclosed the invention.

The evidence in this case thus fulfills the two essential conditions of the on-sale bar. As succinctly stated by Learned Hand:

> "[I]t is a condition upon an inventor's right to a patent that he shall not exploit his discovery competitively after it is ready for patenting; he must content himself with either secrecy, or legal monopoly."

*Metallizing Engineering Co. v. Kenyon Bearing & Auto Parts Co.*, 153 F.2d 516, 520 (C.A.2 1946).

The judgment of the Court of Appeals finds support not only in the text of the statute but also in the basic policies underlying the statutory scheme, including § 102(b). When Pfaff accepted the purchase order for his new sockets prior to April 8, 1981, his invention was ready for patenting. The fact that the manufacturer was able to produce the socket using his detailed drawings and specifications demonstrates this fact. Furthermore, those sockets contained all the elements of the invention claimed in the '377 patent. Therefore, Pfaff's '377 patent is invalid because the invention had been on sale for more than one year in this country before he filed his patent application. Accordingly, the judgment of the Court of Appeals is affirmed.

### *Notes and Questions*

1. *"In public use or on sale."* Are you satisfied that the *Egbert* and the *Moleculon* situations can be distinguished?

Suppose that Nichols had hosted a party for 20-30 guests, during which he demonstrated the puzzle to some of the guests for the purpose of getting feedback about it. Some of the guests picked the puzzle up and inspected it, and Nichols never explicitly asked the guests to maintain the puzzle in secrecy. Same result? See Beachcombers International, Inc. v. WildeWood Creative Products, Inc., 31 F.3d 1154 (Fed.Cir.1994).

Suppose that the applicant/inventor of a new process for making widgets secretly used the process to produce widgets for commercial sale more than a year prior to applying for a patent. The widgets placed on the market did not reveal the process used to make them. Should that use be deemed a "public use" that triggered the § 102(b) one-year statutory bar against the applicant/inventor? The Federal Circuit has held that it should. Kinzenbaw v. Deere and Co., 741 F.2d 383, 390 (Fed.Cir.1984), *cert. denied*, 470 U.S. 1004 (1985). On the other hand, the Federal Circuit has held that a similar secret use by a person unrelated to the applicant does not constitute a public use for purposes of § 102(b) against the applicant. See W.L. Gore & Associates, Inc. v. Garlock, Inc., 721 F.2d 1540, 1550 (Fed.Cir.1983), *cert. denied,* 469 U.S. 851 (1984). Normally, either the applicant's or a third party's public use or sale will trigger the § 102(b) statute of limitations against the applicant. Why should a distinction be made in this case?

If an invention does not yet exist in physical form, how can it be deemed on sale? Why should it be? Is the *Pfaff* "ready to patent" standard likely to provide greater certainty than the Federal Circuit's "substantially complete" standard? How is the "ready to patent" standard likely to affect application filing practices--will inventors generally need to file earlier in the process than under the old "substantially complete" standard?

Under the *Pfaff* decision, what will constitute a "commercial offer for sale"? Must the formal rules of contract law governing "offers" be met, or will more general advertising or promotion suffice? Which approach would make more sense from a policy standpoint? The Federal Circuit has subsequently ruled that actions will only constitute a "commercial offer" for purposes of § 102(b) if they satisfy the formal standards of an offer under the Uniform Commercial Code, allowing another party to create a binding contract for sale with a simple acceptance and consideration. The court reasoned:

> Though the [*Pfaff*] Court did not elaborate on what was meant by "a *commercial* offer for sale"--the issue not being directly presented--the language used strongly suggests that the

> offer must meet the level of an offer for sale in the contract sense, one that would be understood as such in the commercial community. Such a reading leaves no room for "activity which does not rise to the level of a formal 'offer' under contract law principles."
>
> Applying established concepts of contract law, rather than some more amorphous test, implements the broad goal of *Pfaff,* which, in replacing this court's "totality of the circumstances" test with more precise requirements, was to bring greater certainty to the analysis of the on-sale bar. Courts are quite accustomed to and comfortable with determining whether a particular communication or series of communications amounts to an offer in the contract sense, and that type of determination is well established in law.

Group One, Ltd. v. Hallmark Cards, Inc., 254 F.3d 1041, 1046-47 (Fed. Cir. 2001), *cert. denied*, 534 U.S. 1127 (2002).

Aside from technical drawings like the ones at issue in *Pfaff*, what sorts of descriptions might establish that an invention is ready to patent? An inventor's private journal entries? Descriptions of inventive concepts in bids for contracts? An oral description of the invention to a third party? In Robotic Vision Systems, Inc. v. View Engineering, Inc., 249 F.3d 1307 (Fed. Cir.), *cert. denied*, 534 U.S. 1018 (2001), an inventor orally explained his inventive method to a colleague with sufficient specificity that the colleague understood the invention and was able to write the software needed to implement it. The court found that this was sufficient to satisfy the *Pfaff* decision's "ready for patenting" requirement. The Federal Circuit added that it was not necessary that the inventor have complete confidence that his invention would work for its intended purpose: "It will be a rare case indeed in which an inventor has no uncertainty concerning the workability of his invention before he has reduced it to practice. No such requirement will be applied here." *Id.* at 1312.

What would it take to demonstrate that a patented *process* was on sale, for purposes of § 102(b)? See *In re* Kollar, 286 F.3d 1326 (Fed. Cir. 2002) (noting that a process is not sold in the same sense as a tangible item, and thus that sale of know-how describing the process and how to carry it out would not itself trigger the §102(b) statute of limitations. However, sale of a tangible product made by the patented process would constitute a § 102(b) sale.)

2. *Experimental use or sale.* An *experimental* use or sale will not trigger the § 102(b) statute of limitations, even though it may otherwise be "public" in nature. The Supreme Court made this distinction in City of Elizabeth v. American Nicholson Pavement Co., 97 U.S. (7 Otto) 126, 24 L.Ed. 1000 (1877). In that case, the inventor had tested a 75-foot stretch of his new pavement on a well-traveled toll road for six years before applying for a patent. He inspected the pavement regularly and questioned the toll-collector about the public's reaction to it. In upholding the patent, the Court noted:

> The use of an invention by the inventor himself, or by any other person under his direction, by way of experiment, and in order to bring the invention to perfection, has never been regarded as [a public] use. * * *
>
> Now, the nature of a street pavement is such that it cannot be experimented upon satisfactorily except on a highway, which is always public.
>
> [S]uch use is not a public use, within the meaning of the statute, so long as the inventor is engaged, in good faith, in testing its operation. He may see cause to alter it and improve it, or not. His experiments will reveal the fact whether any and what alterations may be necessary. If durability is one of the qualities to be attained, a long period, perhaps years, may be necessary to enable the inventor to discover whether his purpose is accomplished. * * * So long as he does not voluntarily allow others to make it and use it, and so long as it is not on sale for general use, he keeps the invention under his own control, and does not lose his title to a patent.

*Id.*, 97 U.S. (7 Otto) at 134-35. The Court stressed that it made no difference whether, during the period of experimental use, the public incidentally derived a benefit. Nor did it matter that the experimental use revealed how the invention was constructed. The inventor was entitled to take the necessary measures to perfect his invention, and it was in the public's interest that his invention be properly tested before a patent was granted. Since the inventor was engaging in a *bona fide* effort to perfect his invention, and was not using it for profit, the delay in filing did not unfairly prolong his monopoly beyond the period intended by the law.

Following *Elizabeth*, the Court of Appeals for the Federal Circuit found that an orthodontist/inventor did not lose the right to patent his dental appliance by using it on three patients over a period of six years prior to applying for a patent. TP Laboratories, Inc. v. Professional Positioners, Inc., 724 F.2d 965 (Fed.Cir.), *cert. denied*, 469 U.S. 826 (1984). The court noted that disclosure of the appliance to the patients was unavoidable in order to test it, and that while the inventor had failed to obtain pledges of confidentiality from the patients, it was unlikely under the circumstances that the patients would show the appliance to others who would understand its function or want to duplicate it. "In any event, a pledge of confidentiality is indicative of the inventor's continued control which here is established inherently by the dentist-patient relationship of the parties." *Id.*, 724 F.2d at 972. The court concluded:

> A factor in favor of the patentee is that during this critical time the inventor had readily available all of the facilities of TP to commercially exploit the device. Yet, [the devices were not offered for sale to] competing orthodontists despite the fact this was one facet of the inventor's total business activity. Further, the inventor made no extra charge for fitting the three patients with the improved positioners although that in itself is not critical. The facts here indicate the inventor was testing the device, not the market. No commercial exploitation having been made to even a small degree prior to filing the patent application, the underlying policy of prohibiting an extension of the term is clearly not offended in this respect.

> Indeed, none of the policies which underlie the public use bar and which, in effect, define it have been shown to be violated.

*Id.*, 724 F.2d at 972-73.

Contrast *In re* Smith, 714 F.2d 1127 (Fed.Cir.1983). In *Smith*, Airwick conducted a test of the invention (a powder carpet deodorizer) with 76 homemakers more than a year prior to its application for patent. In the first phase of the test, Airwick showed homemakers a video presentation of the product concept, and obtained their reaction to the new product. In the second stage of the test, 40 of the homemakers were given a granular version of the composition and 36 were given a powder version. The homemakers were allowed to use the products in their own homes for about two weeks and were instructed to return any unused portion. Airwick imposed no confidentiality or other restrictions upon them, and made no attempt to control or observe the homemakers' use of the samples. After two weeks, Airwick interviewed 68 of the homemakers, asking, among other things, how the product vacuumed up, whether it deodorized, whether the homemakers had experienced any mechanical problems with their vacuum cleaners, which version the homemakers would buy, and what they would be willing to pay. As Airwick had predicted, the homemakers seemed to favor the powder version over the granular version. There had been some problems with regard to the fragrance. After the test, Airwick continued to work on the product scent and experiment with different product formulations.

The Federal Circuit rejected arguments that Airwick's use was experimental, noting that the experimental use exception to § 102(b) "does not include market testing where the inventor is attempting to gauge consumer demand for his claimed invention. The purpose of such activities is commercial exploitation and not experimentation." *Id.*, 714 F.2d at 1135. The court observed that Airwick could have performed experiments to obtain scientific data on its invention's operation and usefulness in its own laboratories. Its use of "typical housewives" to test the product, without restriction or supervision, indicated that it was seeking information that would assist it to gear its product to maximize potential sales before placing it on the market.

The use of two versions of the product was only meant to determine which version the typical consumer would prefer, not to determine which version was technically superior. The use of the homemaker/consumers to evaluate the fragrance of the product was irrelevant because fragrance strength was not a claimed element of the invention. "It is settled law that the experimental use exception is not applicable to experiments performed with respect to unclaimed features of an invention." *Id.*, 714 F.2d at 1136. As to the continued experimentation with product formulations, the court noted that Airwick already knew that the powdery product would have better antistatic and antisoil properties than the granular type. Since it already knew the technical efficacy of these properties, further tests were not necessary and must have been planned for marketing purposes.

3. *Section 102(c).* Although § 102(c) refers to abandonment of the invention, the case law makes it clear that the provision actually deals with abandonment of the right to a patent. Such abandonment occurs when the inventor expressly or implicitly manifests an intention to relinquish the right to a patent. Courts in early cases used a finding of abandonment to prevent inventors from waiting too long to apply for a patent. For example, in Macbeth-Evans Glass Co. v. General Electric Co., 246 F. 695 (6th Cir.1917), *cert. denied,* 246 U.S. 659 (1918), the inventor of a process for making glass opted to use the process as a trade secret and did so for nearly ten years. At that point he applied for and got a patent. Upon suit to enforce the patent, the court held the patent invalid as abandoned, reasoning that the plaintiff's election of trade secrecy implied a decision to forego a patent, and thus an abandonment. In law, a finding of "abandonment" generally turns on an evaluation of the relevant party's intent. In the § 102(c) context, one must consider whether the evidence indicates that the applicant intended to relinquish a patent. In *Macbeth*, the court acknowledged that the plaintiff might *in fact* have intended to retain the option of a patent as a backup in the event that secrecy later was lost. However, such an intent contemplated "an indefinite delay in disclosure of the invention and a practical and substantial enlargement of any period of monopoly recognized by statute," contrary to a "declared and subsisting public policy." *Id.*, 246 F. at 700. That being the case, the court deemed it appropriate to hold that as a matter of law, the plaintiff was put to an election between a patent and trade

secrecy, and that his choice to pursue trade secrecy would be treated as a decision to forego a patent.

Today, § 102(b) would provide a means of invalidating the patent in *Macbeth*, and in many other instances in which an abandonment might be found within the meaning of § 102(c). As a result, § 102(c) is rarely invoked. Can you think of an instance in which a § 102(c) abandonment might not fall under the § 102(b) statutory bar?

Note that the question of "abandonment" for purposes of § 102(g) differs from the question of "abandonment" for purposes of § 102(c). In the § 102(g) context, the issue is whether the earlier inventor abandoned *the invention*, as opposed to the right to a patent.

4. *Section 102(d).* Section 102(d) requires inventors who have filed for a patent or inventor's certificate abroad to apply promptly for a United States patent. Study the language of subsection (d) closely. When, exactly, does it apply? For an explanation of the scope of subsection (d), see *In re* Kathawala, 9 F.3d 942 (Fed.Cir.1993).

***Problem***

1. In August, 1998, Jones invented a new and innovative can opener. The following October, he made ten prototypes of the can opener and distributed them to ten neighboring households in the suburban neighborhood in which he lived, along with a detailed questionnaire asking the recipients to use the can opener in their homes, then fill out the questionnaire and return it to Jones. Among other things, the questionnaire stated that users should retain the can opener in confidence.

The questionnaire asked users about the conditions under which they used the can opener, the types and sizes of cans opened, the frequency of use, whether they had experienced any difficulties in using the can opener and the specific circumstances in which this had occurred. It also asked them whether they found the size and shape of the opener convenient, and how the can opener compared with other can openers that the recipients had owned or used. Jones collected the questionnaires and, finding that the can opener had worked consistently well for the users under a variety of conditions, decided to market it. He decided to have the can opener manufactured by a Hong Kong manufacturer, import the finished can openers, and distribute them himself to United States purchasers. He began to make inquiries about a Hong Kong manufacturer in January, 1999.

Meanwhile, in February, 1999, Jones attended a two-day kitchen wares exposition in New York. He set up a booth with a videotape player and monitor, and repeatedly played a five-minute videotape in which he described his new can opener and explained how it worked and why it worked better than existing can openers. A number of other kitchen wares producers and retailers saw the videotape. However, while Jones showed a prototype of the can opener on the videotape, he did not bring any of the prototypes with him to the exposition, and did not request or take orders for sales of the can opener. He told retailers visiting his booth that his purpose was merely to notify them that the can opener would be available for sale in the near future, and to give them his business card and collect their business cards.

In January, 2000, Jones received his first shipment of can openers from his Hong Kong manufacturer, and began a sales campaign to kitchen wares retailers and wholesalers. In March, 2000, he filed an application for a U.S. patent. How should his application be treated under Patent Act §102(b)?

### c. The New Section 102: Priority and Novelty under the America Invents Act

As amended by the Leahy-Smith America Invents Act, § 102 provides:

**Section 102. Conditions for Patentability: Novelty**

(a) **Novelty: Prior Art**—A person shall be entitled to a patent unless—

(1) the claimed invention was patented, described in a printed publication, or in public use, on sale, or otherwise available to the public before the effective filing date of the claimed invention; or

(2) the claimed invention was described in a patent issued under section 151, or in an application for patent published or deemed published under section 122(b), in which the patent or application, as the case may be, names another inventor and was effectively filed before the effective filing date of the claimed invention.

(b) **Exceptions**—

(1) DISCLOSURES MADE 1 YEAR OR LESS BEFORE THE EFFECTIVE FILING DATE OF THE CLAIMED INVENTION—A disclosure made 1 year or less before the effective filing date of a claimed invention shall not be prior art to the claimed invention under subsection (a)(1) if—

(A) the disclosure was made by the inventor or joint inventor or by another who obtained the subject matter disclosed directly or indirectly from the inventor or a joint inventor; or

(B) the subject matter disclosed had, before such disclosure, been publicly disclosed by the inventor or a joint inventor or another who obtained the subject matter disclosed directly or indirectly from the inventor or a joint inventor.

(2) DISCLOSURES APPEARING IN APPLICATIONS AND PATENTS—A disclosure shall not be prior art to a claimed invention under subsection (a)(2) if—

(A) the subject matter disclosed was obtained directly or indirectly from the inventor or a joint inventor;

(B) the subject matter disclosed had, before such subject matter was effectively filed under subsection (a)(2), been publicly disclosed by the inventor or a joint inventor or another who obtained the subject matter disclosed directly or indirectly from the inventor or a joint inventor; or

(C) the subject matter disclosed and the claimed invention, not later than the effective filing date of the claimed invention, were owned by the same person or subject to an obligation of assignment to the same person.

(c) **Common Ownership Under Joint Research Agreements**— Subject matter disclosed and a claimed invention shall be deemed to have been owned by the same person or subject to an obligation of assignment to the same person in applying the provisions of subsection (b)(2)(C) if—

(1) the subject matter disclosed was developed and the claimed invention was made by, or on behalf of, 1 or more parties to a joint research agreement that was in effect on or before the effective filing date of the claimed invention;

(2) the claimed invention was made as a result of activities undertaken within the scope of the joint research agreement; and

(3) the application for patent for the claimed invention discloses or is amended to disclose the names of the parties to the joint research agreement.

(d) **Patents and Published Applications Effective as Prior Art**— For purposes of determining whether a patent or application for patent is prior art in a claimed invention under subsection (a)(2), such patent or application shall be considered to have been effectively filed, with respect to any subject matter described in the patent or application—

(1) if paragraph (2) does not apply, as of the actual filing date of the patent or the application for patent; or

(2) if the patent or application for patent is entitled to claim a right of priority under section 119, 365(a), or 365(b), or to claim the benefit of an earlier filing date under section 120, 121, or 365(c), based upon 1 or more prior filed applications for patent, as of the filing date of the earliest such application that describes the subject matter.

Pub. L. No. 112-29 §3(b)(1), 125 Stat 285-87 (2011). The amended § 102 became effective on March 16, 2013, and applies to applications for patent, and resulting patents, effectively filed on or after that date.

## House Report No. 112-98 (Part I)

112th Cong., 1st Sess. 40-43 (2011)

*First Inventor to File*

The ''America Invents Act'' creates a new ''first-inventor-to-file'' system. Every industrialized nation other than the United States uses a patent priority system commonly referred to as ''first-to-file. ''In a first-to-file system, when more than one application claiming the same invention is filed, the priority of a right to a patent is based on the earlier-filed application. The United States, by contrast, currently uses a ''first-to-invent'' system, in which priority is established through a proceeding to determine which applicant actually invented the claimed invention first. Differences between the two systems arise in large part from the date that is most relevant to each respective system. In a first-to-file system, the filing date of the application is most relevant; the filing date of an application is an objective date, simple to determine, for it is listed on the face of the patent. In contrast, in a first-to-invent system, the date the invention claimed in the application was actually invented is the determinative date. Unlike the objective date of filing, the date someone invents something is often uncertain, and, when disputed, typically requires corroborating evidence as part of an adjudication.

There are significant, practical differences between the two systems. Among them is the ease of determining the right to a claimed invention in the instance in which two different people file patent applications for the same invention. In a first-to-file system, the application with the earlier filing date prevails and will be awarded the patent, if one issues. In the first-to-invent system, a lengthy, complex and costly administrative proceeding (called an ''interference proceeding'') must be conducted at the United States Patent and Trademark Office (''USPTO'') to determine who actually invented first. Interference proceedings can take years to complete (even if there is no appeal to the United States Court of Appeals for the Federal Circuit), cost hundreds of thousands of dollars, and require extensive discovery. In addition, because it is always possible that an applicant could be involved in an interference proceeding, companies must maintain extensive recording and document retention systems in case they are later required to prove the date they invented the claimed invention.

Another important difference between the two systems is that in some first-to-file systems, prior art can include the inventor's own disclosure of his invention prior to the filing date of his application. Such systems do not provide the inventor any grace period during which time he is allowed to publish his invention without fear of its later being used against him as prior art. The Committee heard from universities and small inventors, in particular, about the importance of maintaining that grace period in our system. They argued that the grace period affords the necessary time to prepare and file applications, and in some instances, to obtain the necessary funding that enables the inventor to prepare adequately the application. In addition, the grace period benefits the public by encouraging early disclosure of new inventions, regardless of whether an application may later be filed for a patent on it.

Numerous organizations, institutions, and companies have advocated that the U.S. adopt a first-to-file system similar to those used in the rest of the world. The National Academy of Sciences made a similar recommendation after an extensive study of the patent system. When the United States patent system was first adopted, inventors did not typically file in other countries. It is now common for inventors and companies to file for protection in several countries at the same time. Thus, United States applicants, who also want to file abroad, are forced to follow and comply with two different filing systems. Maintaining a filing system so different from the rest of the world disadvantages United States applicants who, in most instances, also file in other countries. A change is long overdue.

Drawing on the best aspects of the two existing systems, the America Invents Act creates a new ''first-inventor-to-file'' system. This new system provides patent applicants in the United States the efficiency benefits of the first-to-file systems used in the rest of the world by moving the U.S. system much closer to a first-to file system and making the filing date that which is most relevant in determining whether an application is patentable. The new system continues, however, to provide inventors the benefit of the 1-year grace period. As part of the transition to a simpler, more efficient first-inventor-to-file system, this provision eliminates costly, complex interference proceedings, because priority will be based on the first application. A new administrative proceeding—called a ''derivation'' proceeding—is created to ensure that the first person to file the application is actually a true inventor. This new proceeding will ensure that a person will not be able to obtain a patent for the invention that he did not actually invent. If a dispute arises as to which of two applicants is a true inventor (as opposed to who invented it first), it will be resolved through an administrative proceeding by the Patent Board. The Act also simplifies how prior art is determined, provides more certainty, and reduces the cost associated with filing and litigating patents.

The Act maintains a 1-year grace period for U.S. applicants. Applicants' own publication or disclosure that occurs within 1 year prior to filing will not act as prior art against their applications. Similarly, disclosure by others during that time based on information obtained (directly or indirectly) from the inventor will not constitute prior art. This 1-year grace period should continue to give U.S. applicants the time they need to prepare and file their applications.

This provision also, and necessarily, modifies the prior-art sections of the patent law. Prior art will be measured from the filing date of the application and will typically include all art that publicly exists prior to the filing date, other than disclosures by the inventor within 1 year of filing. Prior art also will no longer have any geographic limitations. Thus, in section 102 the ''in this country'' limitation as applied to ''public use'' and ''on sale'' is removed, and the phrase ''available to the public'' is added to clarify the broad scope of relevant prior art, as well as to emphasize the fact that it must be publicly accessible. Prior art based on earlier-filed United States applications is maintained, as is current law's grace period, which will apply to all actions by the patent owner during the year prior to filing that would otherwise create § 102(a) prior art. Sections (and subsections) of the existing statute are renumbered, modified, or deleted consistent with converting to a first-inventor-to-file system. Finally, the intent behind the CREATE Act to promote joint research activities is preserved by including a prior art exception for subject matter invented by parties to a joint research agreement. The Act also provides that its enactment of new section 102(c) of title 35 is done with the same intent to promote joint research activities that was expressed in the Cooperative Research and Technology Enhancement Act of 2004 (Public Law 108–453), and that section 102(c) shall be administered in a manner consistent with such intent.

### *Notes and Questions*

*1. Effective filing date.* The America Invents Act makes an applicant's effective filing date the key to novelty. The AIA, § 3(a) amends Patent Act § 100 to provide a definition of the "effective filing date" for a claimed invention in a patent or application for patent:

> (A) if subparagraph (B) does not apply, the actual filing date of the patent or the application for the patent containing a claim to the invention; or
>
> (B) the filing date of the earliest application for which the patent or application is entitled, as to such invention, to a right of priority under section 119, 365(a), or 365(b) or to the benefit of an earlier filing date under section 120, 121, or 365(c).

Pub. L. No. 112-29, 112th Cong., 1st Sess. § 3(a), 125 Stat. 288 (2011). Review the provisions conferring a right to priority or to the benefit of an earlier filing date, listed in subparagraph (B). What do they entail?

*2. Subsection 102(a): Novelty and prior art under the America Invents Act.* How does the new section 102(a) affect the body of "prior art" that may be considered to "anticipate" an applicant's invention? Will the rules regarding identity of invention, discussed in the *VeriSign* case, still apply? Which of the pre-AIA categories of prior art have been deleted from consideration? What categories of prior art have been added?

Presumably the terms "patented" and "described in a printed publication" in the amended § 102 will retain their pre-AIA meaning, as described in case book subsection (a), *supra.* Likewise, "in public use" and "on sale" are likely to retain their earlier meaning, although these two categories of prior art are no longer limited to actions in the United States, and will play a different role in the examination process than they did before. What did Congress have in mind when it provided that a patent will be denied if the claimed invention was "otherwise available to the public?" What does this language add? Could this language be read to limit the meaning of "in public use" and "on sale," for example, when the public use or sale activity does not reveal the invention to the public?

The new § 102(a)(2) generally retains the category of prior art consisting of applications for patent that were pending on the relevant date (now the applicant's filing date) and later published, and patents granted on applications that were pending on the relevant date (formerly incorporated into the prior art through § 102(e)). How will this category augment the "patented" and "described in a printed publication" categories? The new § 102(d) clarifies how we should determine the effective filing date of such potentially anticipating applications. Does the manner of calculating the "effective filing date" of a potentially anticipating application differ from the manner of calculating "effective filing dates" discussed in Note 1, *supra*?

Overall, does the AIA enlarge the body of potentially anticipating prior art, or contract it? What, if any, effect are the new §

102(a) provisions likely to have on inventors' timetable for filing a patent application? Are there any constitutional objections to moving the United States from a first-to-invent to a first-to-file system?

As noted in the House Report, *supra,* the AIA takes precautions to prevent one entity from copying another's invention and obtaining a patent by filing first. America Invents Act §3(i) amends 35 U.S.C. §135 to provide for "derivation proceedings," held before the Patent Trial and Appeals Board. What is likely to be entailed in determining whether one party's invention was "derived" from another's? Is such a proceeding likely to be less complex and expensive than an interference proceeding, to determine which of two parties was the first inventor? Derivation proceedings became available in connection with applications filed on or after March 16, 2013. Interference proceedings (held before the newly named Patent Trial and Appeals Board) will remain available to address priority of invention disputes arising from applications filed prior to that date.

*3. Subsection 102(b): Exceptions to prior art and the new grace period.* "Disclosures" by the applicant's inventor, or by persons deriving the information from the inventor, are excepted from the prior art, if made no more than a year before the applicant's effective filing date. Likewise, the applicant is immune to disclosures by independent third parties, if they are made *after* the inventor or persons deriving from the inventor have already publicly disclosed the same subject matter. Thus, it would appear that priority under the AIA goes to the first inventor to file an application *or* to the first inventor to disclose the invention to the public, assuming that the first discloser files an application within a year of the disclosure. Inventors' ability to block rivals' prior art, and block rivals from obtaining a patent through pre-application disclosure may encourage early, pre-application disclosures. However, disclosing the invention prior to filing an application may disqualify the inventor from obtaining patents abroad, as many countries do not except inventor disclosures from the prior art.

What is meant by the term "disclosure" in § 102(b)? Does it include all of the categories of prior art listed under § 102(a), or does it exclude public use and on sale activity? See 157 Cong. Rec. S5431 (daily ed. Sept. 8, 2011)(statement of Sen. Kyl). Has a person who has made a "disclosure" excepted under § 102(b)(1)(A) "publicly disclosed" the subject matter so as to preclude others' prior art under § 102(b)(1)(B)? Is it possible that some inventor disclosures will themselves be excepted from the prior art, but will not exclude subsequent third-party disclosures from the prior art? Could the opposite be true? Must inventor and inventor-derived disclosures be made within one year of the filing date in order to exclude subsequent third-party disclosures?

What, if any effect will an inventor's experimental use or sale have on patentability, if made more than a year prior to its application date?

*4. The pros and cons of a first-to-file system.* According to the excerpt from the House Report, *supra,* what advantages did Congress see in moving from a first-to-invent to a first-to-file patent priority system? Some commentators have observed that the United States already has a *de facto* first-to-file system, since only a small percentage of applications entail interferences, and when they do, the first applicant to file usually wins. They further note that adopting a first-to-file system will not appreciably change the practice of U.S. inventors, since many U.S. companies, who file both for domestic and foreign patents on new inventions, already plan their patent-filing strategies with foreign first-to-file requirements in mind.

Nonetheless, making the move to a first-to-file priority system was quite controversial, and the subject of years of heated debate, both in Congress and in the patent community. What objections might there be?

Opponents to change have argued that the first-to-invent system is fairer: the first person to invent is more deserving of a patent than the first inventor to file, and the public more readily accepts a system that rewards the first inventor. Moreover, a first-to-file system gives an undue advantage to large companies over individuals, small and start-up companies and academic inventors, who may lack the financial resources to file applications early in the inventive process and win a race to the Patent Office. Opponents also argue that a first-to-file system leads to a decrease in the quality of disclosure in patent applications. The inventor may be rushed to file an application before he has perfected the invention, fully tested it, and ascertained the best mode of practicing it. He is also rushed to file before having an opportunity to explore the commercial value of the invention. The resulting decrease in quality and increase in number of applications, along with the additional prior art entailed in a first-to-file system, will overburden the PTO and affect the quality of its examination process.

What do you think? Canada moved from a first-to-invent to a first-to-file system in 1989. A recent study found a significant drop in the fraction of Canadian patents granted to small inventors coincident with that change. However, the study found no measurable changes in patent quality. David S. Abrams & R. Polk Wagner, *Priority Rules: An Empirical Exploration of First To Invent Versus First To File*, University of Pennsylvania Institute for Law & Economics Research Paper No. 11-29 [draft available at: http://ssrn.com/abstract=1883821] (2011). The AIA addresses the concern about impact on small inventors in several ways. First, AIA § 3(l) calls for a "small business study" to be conducted to examine "the effects of eliminating the use of dates of invention in determining whether an applicant is entitled to a patent". Pub. L. No. 112-29 § 3(l), 125 Stat. 291 (2011). Second, AIA § 10 creates a new category of "micro-entities," who are entitled to a 75% reduction in many of the fees payable to the PTO during the prosecution process. *Id.*, § 10(b). Third, AIA § 28 creates a PTO Ombudsman Program to help small firms navigate the bureaucracy of the patent system. *Id.*,§ 28. Finally, AIA § 29 directs the PTO to "work with and support intellectual property law associations across the country in the establishment of pro bono programs designed to assist financially under-resourced independent inventors and small businesses." *Id.*, § 29. In comments during the Senate debates, Senator Hatch argued that the AIA's transition to a first-inventor-to-file system and establishment of a post-grant review procedure "will decrease litigation costs so that small companies and individuals will not be dissuaded from protecting their patent rights by companies with greater resources." 157 Cong. Rec. S5411 (daily ed., Sept. 8, 2011)(statement of Sen. Hatch). Provisional applications may also assist small entities to secure early filing priority dates without significant expenditure. 35 U.S.C. § 111(b). Is this likely to be sufficient?

## 4. Section 103: Non-Obviousness

* * *

*Pages 217-229 (to Section 6): Replace the materials on these pages with the following:*

### *Notes and Questions*

1. *The obviousness standard.* The obviousness determination distinguishes those inventions that merit the "public embarrassment" of a patent monopoly from those that do not. It is the most difficult standard to satisfy. The *John Deere* Court states that in order to assess the obviousness of an invention under § 103, three basic factual findings must be made: 1) the scope and content of the prior art; 2) the differences between the prior art and the claims at issue; and 3) the level of ordinary skill in the pertinent art. Once these facts are ascertained, then the question of law can be determined: Would the subject matter of the patent application have been obvious to a person having ordinary skill in the art and knowledge of the pertinent prior art? For applications with effective filing dates prior to March 16, 2013 (and patents granted on such applications), this determination must be made as of the applicant's invention date. For applications with effective filing dates on or after March 16, 2013 (and patents granted thereon), the date for determining obviousness is the applicant's effective filing date, to conform to the new first-to-file system.

*a. The scope and content of the prior art.* Patent Act § 102 identifies prior art for purposes of the § 103 obviousness determination. For applications with an effective filing date prior to March 16, 2013, that means that the prior art will include printed publications and patents anywhere in the world, and earlier inventions known or used in the United States, prior to the applicant's invention date. Pre-AIA 35 U.S.C. § 102(a). It will also include inventions revealed in a U.S. patent application that was pending at the time of the invention at issue and was later published or granted. *Id.,* § 102(e). In addition, the prior art will include inventions made in the United States prior to the applicant's and not abandoned, suppressed or concealed, and inventions established in an interference to have been made abroad prior to the applicant's and not abandoned, suppressed or concealed. *Id.,* § 102(g). Finally, the Court of Appeals for the Federal Circuit has held that information the applicant derived from another under the terms of § 102(f) may constitute prior art for purposes of determining the obviousness of the applicant's invention. OddzOn Products, Inc. v. Just Toys, Inc., 122 F.3d 1396 (Fed.Cir.1997). So, for example, if the inventor had information about a prior invention and was influenced by it in making his own invention, that information will be deemed prior art for purposes of evaluating the obviousness of his invention, even though it was not disclosed to the public and would not be prior art against an inventor who had not actually received it.

In the case of applications with an effective filing date on or after March 16, 2013, and patents granted thereon, the prior art will include patents, printed publications, inventions in public use or on sale all over the world, and inventions otherwise available to the public prior to the effective filing date. Pub. L. No. 112-29, §3(b)(1), 125 Stat. 285 (2011). It will also include issued patents and published applications that were pending on the applicant's effective filing date. *Id.* In both the pre-AIA and the post-AIA obviousness determination, two or more pieces of prior art, or "references," may be combined to demonstrate that an invention is obvious.

Pre-AIA § 103(c) limits the use of "secret prior art" against inventors who are working in a collaborative situation. Subsection (c)(1) provides:

> Subject matter developed by another person, which qualifies as prior art only under one or more of subsections (e), (f), and (g) of section 102 of this title, shall not preclude patentability under this section where the subject matter and the claimed invention were, at the time the claimed invention was made,

> owned by the same person or subject to an obligation of assignment to the same person.

Pre-AIA 35 U.S.C. §103(c)(1). This provision was deemed necessary in light of today's large corporate and university research operations, where a range of different researchers may be working on similar or related projects for the same business or academic entity. As long as the invention has not reached the public (under §102(a)), the work of one researcher within the organization will not be used as prior art to render the work of another obvious and unpatentable. In 2004, Congress expanded §103(c) to include secret prior art generated pursuant to a written "joint research agreement," as long as the patent application discloses the names of the parties to the agreement. Thus, the secret prior art generated by researchers pursuant to a joint venture among two or more separate research entities will not constitute prior art for purposes of an obviousness determination, as long as the conditions set forth in § 103(2) and (3) are met. This facilitates useful research partnerships among industry, academia and government agencies by allowing participants to share confidential information about their work. In the America Invents Act, Congress changed these provisions to conform with its new first-to-file and prior art provisions, and moved them from § 103 to § 102. Pub. L. No. 112-29 § 3(b)(1), 125 Stat. 285 (2011). However, it stated an intent to accomplish the same basic purposes as under the pre-AIA law. *Id.,*§ 3(b)(2).

Of course, for purposes of the obviousness determination, only the "pertinent" or "analogous" prior art is considered. Prior art is considered analogous if it is "from the same field of endeavor, regardless of the problem addressed," or if not in the same field as the inventor's endeavor, if it "is reasonably pertinent to the particular problem with which the inventor is involved." *In re* Clay, 966 F.2d 656, 659 (Fed.Cir.1992). The *Clay* case is illustrative. The applicant's invention was a process for storing refined liquid hydrocarbon product in a storage tank having a dead volume between the tank bottom and its outlet port. The process involved preparing a gelatin solution that gelled after it was placed in the tank's dead volume. A prior patent (the Hetherington patent) disclosed an apparatus for displacing dead space liquid using impervious bladders, or large bags, formed with flexible membranes. A second prior patent (the Sydansk patent) disclosed a process for reducing the permeability of hydrocarbon-bearing formations and thus improving oil production, using a gel similar to that used by Clay. The P.T.O. had rejected the Clay application on the finding that while neither prior patent alone rendered the Clay patent obvious, the two in combination did. On appeal, the applicant argued that the Sydansk patent should not have been considered, because it was not analogous.

The Federal Circuit reasoned that the Sydansk patent could not be considered to be within Clay's field of endeavor simply because both related to the petroleum industry: Sydansk taught "the use of a gel in unconfined and irregular volumes within generally underground natural oil-bearing formations to channel flow in a desired direction," while the Clay application taught "the introduction of gel to the confined dead volume of a man-made storage tank." Clay's field of endeavor was "the storage of refined liquid hydrocarbons." The field of endeavor for the Sydansk patent was "the extraction of crude petroleum." *Id.* Nor did the court find the Sydansk patent reasonably pertinent to the problem Clay was trying to solve, so that he might have been motivated to consider it in resolving his own problem:

> Sydansk's gel treatment of underground formations functions to fill anomalies so as to improve flow profiles and sweep efficiencies of injection and production fluids through a formation, while Clay's gel functions to displace liquid product from the dead volume of a storage tank. Sydansk is concerned with plugging formation anomalies so that fluid is subsequently diverted by the gel into the formation matrix, thereby forcing bypassed oil contained in the matrix toward a production well. Sydansk is faced with the problem of recovering oil from rock, *i.e.*, from a matrix which is porous, permeable sedimentary rock of a subterranean formation where water has channeled through formation anomalies and bypassed oil present in the matrix. Such a problem is not reasonably pertinent to the particular problem with which Clay was involved--preventing loss of stored product to tank dead volume while preventing contamination of such product. Moreover, the subterranean formation of Sydansk is not structurally similar to, does not

> operate under the same temperature and pressure as, and does not function like Clay's storage tanks.
>
> * * *
>
> A person having ordinary skill in the art would not reasonably have expected to solve the problem of dead volume in tanks for storing refined petroleum by considering a reference dealing with plugging underground formation anomalies.

*Id.*, 966 F.2d at 659B-0. Compare *In re* Icon Health and Fitness, Inc., 496 F.3d 1374 (Fed. Cir. 2007). In *Icon* the patent claimed a treadmill with a folding base that allowed the base to swivel into an upright storage position. Among other things, the claim called for a gas spring "to assist in stably retaining" the tread base in the upright position. The issue was whether it was appropriate to consider the Teague patent, which disclosed use of a dual-action spring in a bed that folded up into a cabinet, in evaluating the obviousness of the treadmill. While the Federal Circuit acknowledged that the folding bed fell outside the "treadmill art," it held the Teague patent analogous because it was reasonably pertinent to the problem addressed by the treadmill inventor: the need to stably retain a folding mechanism. The court explained:

> "A reference is reasonably pertinent if, even though it may be in a different field from that of the inventor's endeavor, it is one which, because of the matter with which it deals, logically would have commended itself to an inventor's attention in considering his problem." *In re Clay,* 966 F.2d 656, 659 (Fed. Cir. 1992). * * * We therefore have concluded, for example, that an inventor considering a hinge and latch mechanism for portable computers would naturally look to references employing other "housings, hinges, latches, springs, etc.," which in that case came from areas such as "a desktop telephone directory, a piano lid, a kitchen cabinet, a washing machine cabinet, a wooden furniture cabinet, or a two-part housing for storing audio cassettes." *In re Paulsen,* 30 F.3d 1475, 1481-82 (Fed. Cir. 1994).

> Icon's invention provides a treadmill with a folding mechanism and a means for retaining that mechanism in the folded position. The application specifically discusses the gas spring as part of a "lift assistance assembly . . . to apply a force or torque urging the tread base" towards the closed position. Nothing about Icon's folding mechanism requires any particular focus on treadmills; it generally addresses problems of supporting the weight of such a mechanism and providing a stable resting position. Analogous art to Icon's application, when considering the folding mechanism and gas spring limitation, may come from any area describing hinges, springs, latches, counterweights, or other similar mechanisms—such as the folding bed in Teague.

*Id.,* 496 F.3d at 1379-80.

*b. The differences between the prior art and the claims at issue*. To evaluate obviousness, the claimed invention must be evaluated as a whole, taking the total mix of elements into account.

*c. The level of ordinary skill in the pertinent art*. The obviousness determination is made from the perspective of the person having ordinary skill in the art (sometimes called the "PHOSITA"), a fictitious person who is somewhat reminiscent of the ubiquitous "reasonable person" of torts law. In order to make the obviousness evaluation from this person's perspective, one must first determine his or her level of sophistication, skill and knowledge. According to the Court of Appeals for the Federal Circuit:

> Factors that may be considered in determining level of ordinary skill in the art include: (1) the educational level of the inventor; (2) type of problems encountered in the art; (3) prior art solutions to those problems; (4) rapidity with which innovations are made; (5) sophistication of the technology; and (6) educational level of active workers in the field. Not all such factors may be present in every case, and one or more of these or other factors may predominate in a particular case. The important consideration lies in the need to adhere to the statute, i.e., to hold that an invention would or would not have been

> obvious, as a whole, when it was made, to a person of "ordinary skill in the art"--not to the judge, or to a layman, or to those skilled in remote arts, or to geniuses in the art at hand.

Environmental Designs, Ltd. v. Union Oil Co. of California, 713 F.2d 693, 696-97 (Fed.Cir.1983).

A good illustration of the "level of ordinary skill in the art" determination can be found in Daiichi Sankyo Co., Ltd. v. Apotex, Inc., 501 F.3d 1254 (Fed. Cir. 2007), *cert. denied*, 552 U.S. 1185,128 S.Ct. 1259, 170 L.Ed.2d 68 (2008). The invention at issue was a method for treating otopathy (ear infections) with a topical antibiotic without damaging the ear. In evaluating the obviousness of this invention, the district court had concluded that the ordinary person skilled in the art "would have a medical degree, experience treating patients with ear infections, and knowledge of the pharmacology and use of antibiotics. This person would be . . . a pediatrician or general practitioner–those doctors who are often the 'first line of defense' in treating ear infections and who, by virtue of their medical training, possess basic pharmacological knowledge." *Id.* at 1257. The district court went on to find that the claimed invention would not be obvious to such a person, in light of the prior art.

The Court of Appeals for the Federal Circuit reversed, holding that the PHOSITA would have a higher level of skill:

> * * * The inventors of the ' 741 patent were specialists in drug and ear treatments-not general practitioners or pediatricians. At the time of the invention, Inventor Sato was a university professor specializing in otorhinolaryngology; Inventor Handa was a clinical development department manager at Daiichi, where he was involved with new drug development and clinical trials; and Inventor Kitahara was a research scientist at Daiichi engaged in the research and development of antibiotics. Additionally, others working in the same field as the inventors of the '741 patent were of the same skill level. * * *.
>
> Further, the problem the invention of the '741 patent was trying to solve was to create a topical antibiotic compound

> to treat ear infections (otopathy) that did not have damage to the ear as a side effect. Indeed, most of the written description details the inventors' testing ofloxacin on guinea pigs and their findings that ototoxicity did not result from the use of their compound. Such animal testing is traditionally outside the realm of a general practitioner or pediatrician. Finally, while a general practitioner or pediatrician could (and would) prescribe the invention of the '741 patent to treat ear infections, he would not have the training or knowledge to develop the claimed compound absent some specialty training such as that possessed by the '741 patent's inventors. Accordingly, the level of ordinary skill in the art of the '741 patent is that of a person engaged in developing pharmaceutical formulations and treatment methods for the ear or a specialist in ear treatments such as an otologist, otolaryngologist, or otorhinolaryngologist who also has training in pharmaceutical formulations. * * *

*Id.,* at 1257.

While the person from whose perspective the obviousness determination is made has only ordinary skill, that person is deemed to have knowledge of *all* the pertinent prior art.

d. *The legal determination of obviousness based on the findings of fact.* The obviousness determination must be made as of the time the invention was made (or, for applications with effective filing dates on or after March 16, 2013, as of the effective filing date), without the benefit of hindsight. As one practitioner/scholar has pointed out:

> [O]ne must * * * be quite vigilant, lest one commit the insidious sin of "hindsight": one may not use the teachings of the present invention as a guide to interpretation of the prior art, and of what the prior art would suggest to the hypothetical person of ordinary skill in the art, who knows the prior art but not the present invention. * * * [O]f course, the determination of what the prior art would suggest to this hypothetical person is to be made by one who *does* know the present invention, but who is expected to, in a sense, put that knowledge momentarily aside while viewing the prior art through the eyes of the person

> of ordinary skill, while at the same time keeping that knowledge well in mind, since he must recall clearly just *what it is* that the prior art must suggest, in order to render the invention obvious.

Harris, *Prospects for Supreme Court Review of the Federal Circuit Standards for Obviousness of Inventions Combining Old Elements*, 68 J. Pat. & Trademark Off. Soc. 66, 75 (1986).[6]

Most inventions consist of combinations of known elements. Combining two or more prior art references may reveal most or all of the elements the patentee has claimed. Obviousness will turn on whether the PHOSITA would know to combine them in the manner that the patent applicant/holder did. As the Supreme Court explains in *KSR*, the Federal Circuit had gravitated to a standard requiring that the prior art "teach, motivate or suggest" that the combination be made. The Supreme Court finds this approach too narrow and rigid as applied by the Federal Circuit, preferring to ask whether there was an apparent reason for the applicant to combine the constituent elements in the claimed manner. Based on the Court's discussion in *KSR*, what factors should the PTO and courts apply to make this determination? What is the potential impact of the shift in focus? As a matter of public policy, does a "rigid" standard such as the "teach, motivate or suggest" test, or a "flexible" standard, as advocated in *KSR*, make more sense?

In response to the *KSR* opinion, the PTO updated its own examination guidelines. The new guidelines outline seven "Rationales" under which an examiner might reject an applicant's patent claims as obvious:

> (A) Combining prior art elements according to known methods to yield predictable results;
>
> (B) Simple substitution of one known element for another to obtain predictable results;

---

[6] © Robert W. Harris, 1986. Reprinted by permission of the copyright owner.

> (C) Use of a known technique to improve similar devices (methods, or products) in the same way;
>
> (D) Applying a known technique to a known device (method, or product) ready for improvement to yield predictable results;
>
> (E) "Obvious to try"–choosing from a finite number of identified, predictable solutions, with a reasonable expectation of success;
>
> (F) Known work in one field of endeavor may prompt variations of it for use in either the same field or a different one based on design incentives or other market forces, if the variations would have been predictable to one of ordinary skill in the art;
>
> (G) Some teaching, suggestion, or motivation in the prior art that would have led one of ordinary skill to modify the prior art reference or to combine prior art reference teachings to arrive at the claimed invention.

U.S.P.T.O., Examination Guidelines for Determining Obviousness Under 35 U.S.C. 103 in View of the Supreme Court Decision in KSR International Co. v. Teleflex Inc., 72 F.R. 57526 (Oct. 10, 2007).

2. *The secondary considerations.* In *John Deere*, the Supreme Court provided for "secondary considerations" in the obviousness determination:

> Such secondary considerations as commercial success, long felt but unsolved needs, failure of others, etc., might be utilized to give light to the circumstances surrounding the origin of the subject matter sought to be patented. As indicia of obviousness or nonobviousness, these inquiries may have relevancy.

383 U.S. at 17-18. Why should evidence of commercial success, long felt but unsolved needs, or the failure of others be relevant to the determination of obviousness?

While the Court's reference to these considerations as "secondary" suggests that they may not be essential, the Court of Appeals for the Federal Circuit has emphasized their importance. The Federal Circuit has held that evidence relating to the "secondary considerations" (or "objective factors," as the Federal Circuit prefers to call them) must *always* be considered when present, regardless of whether the case is otherwise a close one or not. According to the Federal Circuit, this evidence "may often be the most probative and cogent evidence in the record. It may often establish that an invention appearing to have been obvious in light of the prior art was not." Stratoflex, Inc. v. Aeroquip Corp., 713 F.2d 1530, 1538-39 (Fed.Cir.1983). Moreover, the objective factors may serve "as insurance against the insidious attraction of the siren hindsight when confronted with a difficult task of evaluating the prior art" and may "reassure the decision maker." W.L. Gore & Assoc. v. Garlock, Inc., 721 F.2d 1540, 1553 (Fed.Cir.1983).

Under the Federal Circuit's guidance, the Supreme Court's short list of "secondary considerations" has grown considerably to include such factors as:

(1) movement of the persons skilled in the art in a different direction from that taken by the inventor;

(2) skepticism on the part of experts regarding the approach taken by the inventor;

(3) recognition and acceptance of the patent by competitors who take licenses under it to avail themselves of the merits of the invention; and

(4) the fact that the defendant copied the invention at issue, rather than alternatives in the public domain.

At the same time, the court has stressed that absence of such factors must not be taken as an indication that the invention is obvious. The Federal Circuit has ruled that such absence is a neutral factor.

Of course, a nexus must be demonstrated between objective factor evidence and the issue of obviousness before the evidence can carry any weight. For example, evidence of commercial success may be relevant to prove non-obviousness because marketplace competitors can be expected to take advantage of obvious opportunities for profit. If the commercially successful invention were obvious, persons seeking profit would have made the invention earlier. Before evidence of commercial success can be deemed reliable, however, it must appear that the commercial success was due to the alleged innovative aspects of the invention, and not to such factors as heavy advertisement and sales promotions or to features of the finished product that are not claimed as part of the patented invention.

3. *The mental state of the inventor*. Suppose that an applicant made an invention by mistake (for example, she mistakenly added the wrong ingredient to a composition), or out of ignorance (she expected one result and got a different but useful one). Should the mental state of the inventor make a difference for purposes of determining whether to grant a patent? Should it matter whether the applicant made the invention in a "flash of creative genius" or through long years of methodical trial and error? When it enacted § 103, Congress made it clear that the inventor's mental state is not relevant: "Patentability shall not be negated by the manner in which the invention was made." 35 U.S.C. § 103(a).

*4. Statutory Invention Registrations*. Pre-AIA Patent Act § 157 authorized the PTO to publish a "statutory invention registration" if, among other things, an application satisfied the invention disclosure requirements of § 112 and the inventor waived the right to receive a patent on the invention. Statutory invention registrations were defensive in nature: the registration was effective as prior art for purposes of §§ 102 and 103, and thus prevented later inventors from patenting the same or an obviously similar invention.

The America Invents Act repeals § 157. Thus, as of March 16, 2013, statutory invention registrations can no longer be made. Pub. L. No. 112-29 §3(e), 125 Stat. 287 (2011). Are they needed, give the recently-adopted U.S. practice of publishing patent applications 18 months after they are filed?

5. *The interface between §§ 102(b) and 103.* In Application of Foster, 343 F.2d 980, (CCPA 1965), *cert. denied,* 383 U.S. 966 (1966), Foster filed a patent application on August 21, 1956. The PTO found that an article by Binder, published in August, 1954, rendered Foster's invention obvious. Under pre-AIA law, an applicant's application date was assumed to be his date of invention. However, Foster was able to "swear back" of the Binder article through means of an affidavit demonstrating that he had in fact made his invention prior to December 26, 1952. Since the article was published after Foster's actual invention date, it could not be considered as prior art for purposes of an obviousness evaluation under Pre-AIA § 103. The Court of Customs and Patent Appeals nonetheless found that the article disqualified Foster from obtaining a patent, because the Binder article was published more than one year prior to Foster's U.S. filing date. Foster was disqualified under the §102(b) statutory bar, even though the article did not anticipate his invention but only rendered it obvious.

The court reasoned that the purpose of § 102(b) was to encourage diligence in filing patent applications by requiring that the application be filed within a year after disclosure of the invention to the public through one of the four means enumerated that section. An invention may be fully disclosed through publication of an article that precisely anticipates the invention, or through a publication that, when combined with preexisting knowledge, renders the invention obvious to persons skilled in the art. The question should be whether the event placed the invention in the public domain, either by anticipating it or rendering it obvious. If it did, the § 102(b) statute of limitations should start to run.

The Court of Appeals for the Federal Circuit has continued to hold (in cases involving pre-AIA law) that when patents, printed publications, public use and on sale events that (either by themselves or in combination with ordinary skill or other prior art references) render an invention obvious, they trigger the § 102(b) statutory bar. Thus, an applicant who qualifies for a patent under §103 may *lose* his right to a patent if the invention becomes obvious later on and the applicant fails to file his application within the one-year period specified in §102(b).

The AIA's move to a first-to-file system renders "swearing back" irrelevant for patent applications with effective filing dates on or after March 16, 2013. However, swearing back will continue to be available for applications and patents with earlier effective filing dates, as will the practice of triggering the § 102(b) statutory bar when one of the forms of disclosure listed in that section renders an applicant's invention obvious.

### *Problems*

1. In 2008, Mary conceived and reduced to practice a novel, non-obvious machine for weaving fine fabric. She then began to work on developing a loom and a mechanical arm device, which would be used in connection with the machine, and sold with the machine as a package. It took Mary two years to perfect the loom and mechanical arm, and another six months to make the necessary preparations to begin mass producing the three components and put them on the market. Mary introduced the machine, loom and mechanical arm device, as a package, to the market in October, 2011. The loom and mechanical arm device are not patentable, but the machine is not usable without them. Mary has not sought to patent the machine.

In 2010, Jane invented a weaving machine that, while not exactly the same as Mary's, was obvious in light of Mary's machine. Under pre-AIA law, will Jane be able to obtain a patent under Patent Act § 103? Would that result change under the AIA?

2. Jim invented a new type of widget in Australia in 2008, but did not take any steps to market or patent it, or publish any description of it. A year later, Jim demonstrated the new widget to Mark, a U.S. widget producer, who was visiting Jim's Australian laboratory. Mark later returned to the U.S. and commenced work on a new type of widget. In making his invention, Mark was influenced by Jim's widget. Mark later applied for a patent for the new widget he developed. Under pre-AIA law, should Jim's earlier Australian widget be considered as prior art in evaluating the obviousness of Mark's widget? Would Jim's widget be deemed relevant under the AIA?

3. In the year 2005, in Paris, Pierre invented a new composition of matter that was especially effective in removing grease stains. He applied for a French patent in May, 2006, and a U.S. patent in August, 2006. The U.S. PTO published Pierre's application in November, 2007, but Pierre subsequently abandoned his application, so that a U.S. patent was never granted. Pierre was granted a French Patent in June, 2008. Jennifer invented a composition of matter that was obvious in light of Pierre's in the U.S. in September, 2006, and applied for a patent in 2007. Could Pierre's invention be considered as prior art in evaluating the patentability of Jennifer's, under either pre-or post-AIA?

## 6. Section 112: Disclosure

*Page 237: Add the following to the end of Note 3:*

In America Invents Act § 15, Pub. L. No. 112-29 § 15, 125 Stat. 328 (2011), Congress amended Patent Act § 282 to provide that "failure to disclose the best mode shall not be a basis on which any claim of a patent may be canceled or held invalid or otherwise unenforceable." This amendment became effective on September 16, 2011, and applies to proceedings commenced on or after that date. However, while failure to disclose the best mode is no longer a ground for invalidating an issued patent, or defending against an infringement claim, disclosing the best mode remains a requirement that patentees must meet under Patent Act § 112. Compliance with the best mode requirement will remain subject to review by the PTO during prosecution, although the P.T.O. does not frequently reject an application for failure to satisfy the best mode requirement.

What led Congress to make this amendment? Elimination of the best mode requirement had been discussed for a number of years. First, most countries, while requiring enabling disclosure, do not require disclosure of the best mode. Deleting the requirement as a ground for cancellation, invalidity or unenforceability brings the United States closer to the international norm. Second, critics perceived that the best mode defense was being used as a litigation tactic. Asserting the best mode defense enabled a party to pursue burdensome discovery regarding the inventor's "subjective beliefs" prior to filing. Due to the subjective nature of the inquiry, and the wide range of circumstances that might support a finding of failure to disclose the best mode, it was difficult for the patentee to discredit and dismiss best mode challenges early in the litigation. Finally, the best mode the inventor contemplates at the time of filing is of questionable value, since the best mode is likely to change over time.

*Page 240: Insert the following after 37 C.F.R. § 1.56 (2009):*

On July 21, 2011, the P.T.O. gave notice of proposed rule-making to adopt a higher standard for determining whether information is "material" and thus subject to the § 1.56 disclosure requirement. 76 Fed. Reg. No. 140, 43631 (July 21, 2011). For more information about this, see revisions to pages 340-341, *supra.*

## 7. Inventorship

*Pages 240-242: Replace the text of Section 7. Inventorship with the following:*

The Patent Act makes it clear that the *inventor* is entitled to a patent, even though the inventor may assign his right, and frequently does.[7] See, *e.g.,* 35 U.S.C. § 101 ("whoever invents or discovers any

[7] The general rules regarding the ownership of an invention made by an employee during the course of employment are discussed in Chapter Two, *supra.* For example, if the employee/inventor was hired to do the research that leads to the invention, the common law may imply an assignment of ownership by the employee to the employer. Even if the common law would designate the employee as the owner of the invention, the employee may have signed an express agreement assigning to the employer in advance the rights in any inventions he makes while employed.

new and useful process, machine, manufacture, or composition of matter * * * may obtain a patent.").

When an invention is made by two or more persons jointly, they must apply for a patent jointly. 35 U.S.C. § 116. When will persons qualify as joint inventors? First, each person claiming to be a joint inventor must have contributed to the final concept of the invention. Nartron Corp. v. Schukra U.S.A., Inc., 558 F.3d 1352 (Fed. Cir. 2009). One does not become a joint inventor merely by explaining well-known principles or concepts, or the state of the art to the inventor. Moreover, the joint inventor must "make a contribution to the claimed invention that is not insignificant in quality, when that contribution is measured against the dimension of the full invention." *Id.,* at 1356-57.

In addition, the purported joint inventors must have *collaborated* with one another. Kimberly-Clark Corp. v. Procter & Gamble Distributing Co., Inc., 973 F.2d 911 (Fed.Cir.1992), is illustrative. In 1979 and 1982, Buell, a Procter & Gamble employee, made a disposable diaper with inner flaps to control leakage. In 1982, Enloe, a Kimberly-Clark employee, conceived of a disposable diaper with inner flaps. Enloe's work led to the issuance of a patent to Kimberly-Clark. In 1985, Lawson, a Proctor & Gamble employee, conceived of a disposable diaper that used inner flaps. Lawson worked alone on the invention, unaware of Buell's earlier work. (At the time, Buell was likewise unaware of Lawson.) Procter & Gamble, as Lawson's assignee, filed a patent application naming Lawson as the sole inventor and later obtained a patent.

The issue of priority arose in subsequent litigation between Procter & Gamble and Kimberly-Clark. Procter & Gamble asserted that the Lawson patent had priority over the Kimberly-Clark patent, on the grounds that Buell and Lawson were joint inventors, and Buell's work marked the actual date of conception for the Procter & Gamble diaper. Pursuant to 35 U.S.C. § 256, Procter & Gamble asked the court to order that the omission of Buell as an inventor in the Lawson patent be corrected. The district court found that Buell and Lawson were not joint inventors, and the Court of Appeals for the Federal Circuit affirmed.

The Federal Circuit found that Congress, in amending Patent Act § 116 in 1984, intended to codify the principles set forth in Monsanto Co. v. Kamp, 269 F.Supp. 818, 824 (D.D.C.1967). The *Monsanto* opinion had stated:

> A joint invention is the product of *collaboration* of the inventive endeavors of two or more persons *working toward the same end* and producing an invention by their *aggregate* efforts. To constitute a joint invention, it is necessary that each of the inventors work on the same subject matter and make some contribution to the inventive thought and to the final result. Each needs to perform but a part of the task if an invention emerges from all of the steps taken together. It is not necessary that the entire inventive concept should occur to each of the joint inventors, or that the two should physically work on the project together. One may take a step at one time, the other an approach at different times. One may do more of the experimental work while the other makes suggestions from time to time. The fact that each of the inventors plays a different role and that the contribution of one may not be as great as that of another does not detract from the fact that the invention is joint if each makes some original contribution, though partial, to the final solution of the problem.

*Monsanto*, 269 F.Supp. at 824.

In finding that the Procter & Gamble employees, Buell and Lawson, were not joint inventors, the Federal Circuit explained:

> What is clear is that the statutory word "jointly" is not mere surplusage. For persons to be joint inventors under Section 116, there must be some element of joint behavior, such as collaboration or working under common direction, one inventor seeing a relevant report and building upon it or hearing another's suggestion at a meeting. Here there was nothing of that nature. Individuals cannot be joint inventors if they are completely ignorant of what each other has done until

> years after their individual independent efforts. They cannot be totally independent of each other and be joint inventors.

*Kimberly-Clark*, 973 F.2d at 916-17.

In the absence of an assignment or an agreement to the contrary, each joint inventor is a joint owner of the patent, and each joint owner may exploit the patented invention freely without the consent of the other joint owners, and without accounting to them. 35 U.S.C. § 262.

## 8. International Considerations

*Pages 242-249: Replace the text of Subsection 8. International Considerations with the following:*

*Comparative Considerations*

Many similarities exist among the patent laws of the various nations. For example, foreign patent laws generally require that inventions be novel, non-obvious and useful in order to qualify for a patent, though each of these requirements may differ somewhat in nomenclature, scope, and detail from its counterpart in United States law. Perhaps the most important *difference* between the U.S. and other nations' patent laws has been the United States' emphasis on granting a patent to the first person to invent, rather than the first inventor to file an application. (This gap has finally been narrowed through the United States' adoption of the America Invents Act.) Another important difference is that most other nations lack a "grace period" comparable to that available to United States patent applicants: In many countries, virtually any introduction of the invention to the public via commercial activity or publication, either domestically or abroad, prior to the filing date will disqualify the invention. This poses a trap for unwary United States inventors--while taking advantage of the U.S. grace period, they may disqualify themselves for patents in much of the rest of the world. In addition, many countries do not require an applicant to disclose the "best mode" of carrying out her invention, as the U.S. does in Patent Act § 112. In these countries, the applicant need only adequately disclose one mode of carrying out the invention.

Traditionally, the duration of patent protection has differed from one country to the next. Countries have also differed significantly in the scope of subject matter deemed eligible for patent protection. While the United States has tended to offer patent protection for a very wide range of inventions ("anything under the sun that is made by man"), many developing nations, in particular, have denied patents for agricultural chemicals and pharmaceutical inventions, deeming a monopoly (and the ability to charge monopoly prices) to be contrary to the national interest. This refusal has led to considerable dissatisfaction on the part of U.S. drug and chemical industries, who have had to compete with replicas of their own innovative inventions abroad.

*Multinational Filings*

Needless to say, variations in national patent laws are not conducive to obtaining global patent protection for a new invention. A company wishing to launch a global marketing campaign for an invention must apply for a patent in each country in which it plans to do business. Understanding and satisfying the substantive and procedural variations in each nation's patent laws can be difficult and expensive. A number of attempts have been made to ease this process.

*1. The Paris Convention.* The Paris Convention for the Protection of Industrial Property[8] was a first step. A multinational treaty with over 170 members (including the U.S.), the Paris Convention is founded on national treatment: it essentially obligates each member to provide as great patent protection to the nationals of other member nations as it provides to its own nationals. While this gets the foreign applicant's foot in the door, it does not guarantee a high level of substantive patent protection: The Paris Convention prohibits discrimination, but imposes relatively few standards

[8] Paris Convention for the Protection of Industrial Property, July 14, 1967, 21 U.S.T. 1629, 982 U.N.T.S. 369.

regarding the scope or extent of substantive protection that member nations must provide. Nor does the Paris Convention attempt to standardize member nations' patent application procedures.

Even though it does relatively little to harmonize national patent laws, the Paris Convention makes multinational filings easier through its foreign filing priority provision. Article 4 of the Paris Convention provides that a person who files an application for patent in any member country can claim his filing date in that country in subsequent filings in other member countries during the next twelve months. So, for example, if X Company files a patent application in member country #1 on January 1, 2012, all of the patent applications that it files in other member countries during the next twelve months will have an effective filing date of January 1, 2012.

The usefulness of this provision is made clear in art. 4(B):

> [A]ny subsequent filing in any of the other countries of the Union before the expiration of the [twelve-month] period * * * shall not be invalidated by reason of any acts accomplished in the interval, in particular, another filing, the publication or exploitation of the invention * * *.

Recall that most foreign countries grant patents to the first inventor to file, and lack the one-year "grace period" afforded to inventors under U.S. Patent Act § 102. Assume that X files in country #1 on January 1, 2012. Y makes the same invention and files for a patent in country #2 in August, 2012. Z publishes a paper disclosing the invention in October, 2012. X then files for a patent in country #2 in December, 2012. In the absence of Paris Convention article 4, both Y and Z's actions are likely to disqualify X from obtaining a patent in country #2, because they occurred prior to his filing date. However, because of article 4, country #2 will treat X's application as though it were filed on January 1, his filing date in country #1. X will be saved from the consequences of the intervening actions of Y and Z.

Article 4 thus gives an inventor some flexibility. As long as he files an application in one member country (which may be his own country), the inventor can take up to twelve months to test the marketability of the invention, and make the necessary preparations for foreign filings, without fear of losing his patent opportunities abroad in the interim. The substance of art. 4 is implemented in §119 of the United States Patent Act.

2. *The Patent Cooperation Treaty.* The Patent Cooperation Treaty ("PCT")[9] was an important second step in aiding the procurement of international patent protection. The PCT simplifies international patent filings by providing a centralized means of filing patent applications for a number of countries simultaneously. Administered by the International Bureau of the World Intellectual Property Organization ("WIPO"),[10] the PCT now has over 140 members, including the U.S. and most other developed nations.

The PCT entitles nationals or residents of member nations to file "international applications" for patents. They may do this by simply filing a standardized international application with their home patent office, which designates all the other PCT member nations in which the applicant wishes to file. The applicant generally files in his own language and pays a fee in his own nation's currency. The receiving office checks to see that the application is in proper form and, if it is, assigns an international filing date, which will be either the date of a qualifying earlier filing under the Paris Convention or the date of the international filing itself. The effect of this is essentially the same as if a patent application had been filed with the national patent office of each designated member nation on that date. The application is then forwarded (if necessary) to an international searching authority, which conducts an international search of the relevant prior art. The United States' PTO is one of the international searching authorities.

---

[9] Patent Cooperation Treaty, June 19, 1970, 28 U.S.T. 7645, 1037 U.N.T.S. 213.

[10] The World Intellectual Property Organization is a specialized agency of the United Nations, whose objective is to promote the protection of intellectual property throughout the world. It administers the Paris Convention and the PCT, as well as a number of other intellectual property treaties.

The search authority examines published patent documents and technical literature, and produces an international search report.

This search report gives the applicant a good sense of how likely he is to obtain a patent. The applicant then has the opportunity to amend his claims in order to avoid the prior art that has been found, or withdraw his application altogether, if he finds proceeding impractical in light of the search results. If the application is not withdrawn, it is published 18 months after the international filing date. By the end of the twentieth month, the application must be sent to the patent office of each of the designated nations in which a patent is sought. This begins the "national stage" of the process.

At this point, the applicant must send national fees to each national office and supply a translation of the application whenever required. He may need to hire local counsel to prosecute the patent in each national patent office. Each nation proceeds to apply its own law to determine whether a patent will be granted.

If the applicant chooses, directly after the international search and before the application is sent to the national patent offices, he can request an international preliminary examination. The purpose of this examination is to produce a nonbinding opinion about the novelty, inventiveness and industrial applicability of the invention.[11] While the preliminary examination is not binding on the national offices, it is generally highly regarded and thus is persuasive. When the preliminary examination is requested, this adds an additional ten months before the application must be sent to the designated national patent offices, initiating the "national stage."

Even though the PCT procedure does not avoid the cost and difficulty of prosecuting the application before each of the individual national patent offices, it nonetheless has proved popular, and is

---

[11]Novelty, inventiveness and industrial applicability are the international criteria for patentability. They are conceptually similar to the U.S. requirements of novelty, nonobviousness and usefulness.

widely perceived as offering important advantages to international patent applicants. One of the most important perceived advantages is the period of time that it provides between the initial application and the point at which national fees and translations are due and appearances must be made before the individual national offices. This permits applicants to reserve their patent priority in a potentially large number of countries, while testing the commercial viability of their inventions. If the commercial prospects are not promising, they may discontinue prosecution prior to the national stage, avoiding the considerable cost and effort that the national stage entails.

Another advantage, of course, is that the applications can all be prepared in the same format. Applications meeting the form and content requirements of the PCT must be accepted in all member nations, though the nations may impose different requirements for direct applications. There may also be a savings of attorney time, as amendments to the claims can be made during the centralized international phase, avoiding duplicative actions in the various national offices.

The PCT is implemented in ' ' 351-76 of the United States' Patent Act.[12]

*3. Other Efforts: the Patent Law Treaty and TRIPs.* As international marketing of goods and services has become increasingly common, many nations have sought additional ways to harmonize the patent laws of the world. In the late 1980's and early 1990's a number of interested nations met, under the auspices of the World Intellectual Property Organization ("WIPO"), to attempt to draft a treaty establishing global *substantive* patent standards, including a uniform rule regarding patent priority, a uniform grace period, and disclosure requirements. See Moy, *The History of the Patent Harmonization*

---

[12]Another international patent agreement to which the U.S. adheres, the Strasbourg Agreement Concerning the International Patent Classification, March 24, 1971, 26 U.S.T. 1793, T.I.A.S. 8140, eases the international prior art search by imposing an international classification system for patented subject matter.

*Treaty: Economic Self-Interest as an Influence*, 26 J. Marshall L. Rev. 457 (1993); Fiorito, *The "Basic Proposal" for Harmonization of U.S. and Worldwide Patent Laws Submitted by WIPO*, 73 J. Pat. & Trademark Off. Soc. 83 (1991). While these efforts ultimately failed, negotiators were able to conclude a treaty (the Patent Law Treaty)[13] further harmonizing procedural filing requirements. Nations ratifying the new WIPO Patent Law Treaty accept standardized patent application forms (in the case of applications filed outside of the PCT process, which is already standardized), eliminate some unduly complex and expensive formalities that have been imposed in the past, provide relief and reinstatement of rights when applicants and patentees miss certain deadlines, and take other steps to conform their patent application process to international norms. The Patent Law Treaty thus further reduces the complexity and cost of obtaining international patent protection.

On another front, efforts were made in the late 1980's and early 1990's to bring minimum substantive standards of patent protection into the General Agreement on Tariffs and Trade ("GATT"), the leading world agreement regulating international trade. These efforts met with significant success. Among other things, the resulting Agreement on Trade Related Aspects of Intellectual Property Rights, Including Trade in Counterfeited Goods ("TRIPs" Agreement) harmonizes national laws regarding the term of patent protection, the scope of patentable subject matter, and the substantive rights and remedies to be provided to patentees.[14]

---

[13]Patent Law Treaty, Adopted at Geneva, June 1, 2000, 39 I.L.M. 1047. The United States ratified the Patent Law Treaty in December, 2012, and enacted implementing legislation in 2012. See Patent Law Treaties Implementation Act of 2012, P.L. No. 112-211, 126 Stat. 1527 (2012).

[14]For further discussion of the TRIPs Agreement, see Chapter One, *supra*.

--The TRIPs Agreement provides that the term of patent protection must not end "before the expiration of a period of twenty years counted from the filing date." TRIPs, Art. 33.[15]

--TRIPs art. 28 specifies minimum rights that member countries must afford patentees: patentees must enjoy rights against the unauthorized "making, using, offering for sale, selling or importing" of their patented products. Process patents must convey the right to prevent unauthorized use of the process and the use, offer for sale, sale or importation of products obtained directly through the process.[16] The TRIPs agreement also places important limitations on members' ability to impose compulsory licenses and patent forfeiture.

---

[15]In accepting the Uruguay Round and joining the newly formed World Trade Organization ("WTO"), the United States was required to implement this term, in place of a patent term of 17 years counted from the date the patent issues, which it traditionally had provided. As amended, Patent Act §154(a)(2) specifies that United States patent protection begins on the date the patent is issued and ends 20 years from the date on which the application for patent was filed *in the United States*. 35 U.S.C. § 154(a)(2). The term is not to be measured by reference to an earlier Paris Convention foreign filing priority date. Should the foreign filing of a PCT application that designates the United States trigger the 20-year term? See 35 U.S.C.A. § 363.

As will be discussed in the next Section, the U.S. has subsequently amended its Patent Act to provide for publication of many patent applications 18 months after their filing date. It has added a complimentary provision providing limited rights to patentees during the interim between the date their application is published and the date their patent issues. 35 U.S.C. § 154(d).

[16]This provision also necessitated amendments to the United States Patent Act. Uruguay Round Agreements Act. See 35 U.S.C. §§ 154(a), 271 (a). Prior to the amendment, the U.S. had not recognized a patentee's right to prevent an offer for sale or the importation of its patented invention, or of products of its patented process.

--TRIPs article 27 provides for a broad range of patentable subject matter, that requires many nations to extend protection to categories of inventions they had previously excluded: "patents shall be available for any inventions, whether products or processes, in all fields of technology, provided that they are new, involve an inventive step and are capable of industrial application." There are some limitations on this broad provision, however: member nations may exclude from patentability

(1) inventions whose commercial exploitation threatens "*ordre public* or morality, including to protect human, animal or plant life or health or to avoid serious prejudice to the environment;"

(2) "diagnostic, therapeutic and surgical methods for the treatment of humans or animals;" and

(3) "plants and animals other than microorganisms, and essentially biological processes for the production of plants or animals other than nonbiological and microbiological processes." *Id.*

# D. THE PATENTING PROCESS

* * *

## 2. Patent Prosecution and Related Procedures

*Pages 253-258: Replace the text of Subsection 2, Patent Prosecution and Related Procedures, with the following:*

**2. Patent Prosecution and Related Procedures**

An application for patent must include 1) a written specification, as prescribed under Patent Act §112; 2) a drawing, as required under § 113; and 3) an oath or declaration as prescribed in § 115. The application must be accompanied by a filing fee. 35 U.S.C. § 111(a). In the past, the Patent Act required that the inventor file the application for patent. The America Invents Act provides that the inventor must be named in the application. However, § 118, as amended, will permit a person to whom the inventor has assigned or is under an obligation to assign the invention to apply for the patent, in the inventor's place. When the inventor is unavailable to provide the oath or declaration described above, the applicant will be permitted to file a "substitute statement." 35 U.S.C. § 115.

Inventors/assignees who wish to obtain an early filing date, but are unable or do not wish to make a full filing, may file a "provisional application." To make a provisional application, the inventor must file a written description of the invention, and drawings, but need not submit claims or an oath/declaration. The provisional application is not examined on its merits, and the filing fee is significantly lower than the fee for non-provisional applications. Once the applicant has filed a provisional application, she has up to twelve months to file a non-provisional application, complete with claims. Once it is filed, the non-provisional application receives the benefit of the earlier, provisional application filing date,[17] and proceeds to examination. 35 U.S.C. § 111(b).

The application is assigned for examination to the P.T.O. examining group that works with the area of technology most nearly

---

[17] A patent endures for a term of 20 years measured from the filing date. The filing date used for purposes of measuring the term is the non-provisional application filing date, not the provisional filing date. This gives strictly domestic applicants an advantage similar to the advantage that foreign applicants get under the Paris Convention when they rely on their earlier foreign filing date as their official U.S. filing date. (In that case, the foreign applicant's U.S. patent term is measured from the actual U.S. filing date, not from the claimed foreign filing date.)

related to the claimed invention. The assigned examiner searches U.S. and foreign patent documents and other available published literature to determine whether the claimed invention is novel and non-obvious, and studies the application for compliance with all of the legal requirements set forth in the Patent Act and the P.T.O. rules of practice. The examiner notifies the applicant in writing of his initial decision. (This notification is called the first "office action," and generally will occur within 14 months.) If the initial decision is adverse, the notice states the reasons, and provides information or references to assist the applicant in evaluating whether to continue prosecuting the application. It is common for some or all of an applicant's claims to be rejected in the first office action. Relatively few applications are allowed as initially claimed. U.S. Patent and Trademark Office, General Information Concerning Patents (2005).[18]

As a result of amendments to Patent Act § 122 which became effective in 2000, a non-provisional utility patent application generally will be published during the course of the examination process--eighteen months after its earliest filing date.[19] However, the applicant may request that the application not be published if the applicant certifies that she has not and will not file an application to patent the invention in another country (or pursuant to an international agreement) that requires publication. Most other countries do publish applications 18 months after they are filed. Thus, § 122(b) essentially provides that if the applicant is not subjecting herself to publication by filing abroad, she can avoid having her domestic application published, and retain the trade secrecy status of the invention up to the point that the patent is issued (or if the application ultimately is rejected, indefinitely). What are the advantages of publishing applications 18 months after their filing date? After the application is published, the America Invents Act permits interested members of the public to submit patents, published patent applications, or other printed publications of potential relevance to the examination for

[18] This publication can be found on the PTO's web site: http://www.uspto.gov.

[19] The publication provisions took effect on November 29, 2000, and apply to all patent applications filed thereafter.

consideration and inclusion in the record. They must accompany the submission with a concise statement of why the submitted prior art is relevant. Pub. L. No. 112-29 § 8, 125 Stat. 315 (2011) (amending 35 U.S.C. § 122(e)).[20]

After being rejected in the first office action, the applicant may request reconsideration in writing, pointing out any alleged errors in the examiner's action, and responding to the examiner's objections. She may also amend the application, pointing out why she thinks the amended claims are patentable in view of the prior art the examiner cited in his initial rejection. After the applicant's reply, the examiner will reconsider the application and notify her of his determination, as in the first office action. This second office action usually will be made final. PTO, General Information, *supra*. If the patent application is found allowable, the P.T.O. notifies the applicant. The applicant must then pay an issue fee. The patent is issued either to the applicant or her assignee, and the patent file is opened to the public. The patentee must pay periodic maintenance fees to maintain the patent in force. *Id.*

An applicant may appeal rejection to the Patent Trial and Appeal Board (formerly the Board of Patent Appeals and Interferences) which now consists of the P.T.O.'s Director, Deputy Director, the Commissioner for Patents, the Commissioner for Trademarks, and administrative patent judges. Normally an appeal is heard by only three members. As an alternative to appeal, when an applicant desires consideration of different claims or further evidence, she may file a continuation application. A continuation application is essentially a new application. However, if it is filed before expiration of the period for appeal, makes specific reference to the earlier application, and complies with other requirements, the continuation application will be entitled to the earlier application's filing date. *Id.*

---

[20] The PTO commenced accepting these pre-issuance submissions September 16, 2012. There is a limited window of time in the examination process in which the submissions will be accepted.

If the Patent Trial and Appeal Board decides the applicant's appeal adversely to the applicant, she may appeal the decision directly, on the record generated in the P.T.O., to the Court of Appeals for the Federal Circuit.[22] 35 U.S.C. § 141. Alternatively, she may file a civil action against the P.T.O. Director in the United States District Court for the Eastern District of Virginia, seeking judgment that she is entitled to receive a patent.[23] 35 U.S.C. §145.

*Interferences and Derivation Proceedings*

Sometimes, under the first-to-invent priority system, two or more applications have been filed claiming substantially the same patentable invention. Since only one applicant/inventor may obtain a patent for the invention, the P.T.O. has instituted a proceeding, called an "interference," to determine which of the inventors was the first and thus entitled to the patent. Interference proceedings could also arise between an application and a patent already issued, if the application was filed within a year of the issued patent's issuance and/or publication, and the conflicting application was not barred for some other reason. 35 U.S.C. § 135. The P.T.O. estimates that about one percent of patent applications have been Interference proceedings are notorious for their complexity and expense.

---

[22] In Dickinson v. Zurko, 527 U.S. 150, 119 S.Ct. 1816, 144 L.Ed.2d 143 (1999), the United States Supreme Court addressed the standard of review that the court of appeals for the Federal Circuit should use in reviewing the P.T.O.'s findings of fact in denying an application. The Supreme Court held that when the patent applicant appeals directly to the court of appeals on the record, the court of appeals must apply the standard set forth in the Administrative Procedure Act. Under this standard, the court of appeals may only set aside P.T.O. fact findings if they are arbitrary, capricious, or an abuse of discretion, or if they are unsupported by substantial evidence.

[23] When a dissatisfied applicant brings suit in district court under 35 U.S.C. § 145, it may introduce evidence of patentability that was not presented to the P.T.O. Kappos v. Hyatt, __ U.S. __, 132 S.Ct. 1690 (2012).

With the United States' move to a first-to-file system, interferences will no longer be necessary. However, there will be a phase-out period in which interference procedures remain available in connection with patents and applications with effective filing dates prior to March 16, 2013. These remaining interferences will be heard by the newly named Patent Trial and Appeal Board, which will apply the law as it existed immediately before March 16, 2013.

With the new first-to-file system, a new administrative proceeding, called a "derivation proceeding" comes to the fore. Derivation proceedings, before the Patent Trial and Appeal Board, will resolve disputes over whether an applicant is a true inventor, or merely derived its invention from another source. Under newly amended Patent Act § 135, an applicant for patent may file a petition to institute a derivation proceeding, demonstrating that an inventor named in an earlier application derived the claimed invention from an inventor named in the petitioner's application and filed the earlier application without authorization. The petition must be filed within a year following first publication of the derived subject matter. A party who is dissatisfied with the Board's resolution of a derivation proceeding may appeal to the Court of Appeals for the Federal Circuit or opt to file a civil action in district court. Pub. L. No. 112-29 §3(i), (j), 125 Stat. 289, 90 (2011) (amending 35 U.S.C. §§ 141, 146, effective 3/16/13.) AIA § 3(h) amends 35 U.S.C. § 291 to permit civil action against the owner of another patent that claims the same invention and has an earlier effective filing date, if that invention was derived from the plaintiff's inventor. This action must be filed within a year from the date the first patent issued. Pub. L. No. 112-29 § 3(h), 125 Stat. 288 (2011).

### *Reissuance*

When an issued patent is defective in its specification or drawing, or because the patentee claimed more or less than he had a right to claim, the patentee may request a reissue of the patent in corrected form. (No reissued patent can be granted enlarging the scope of the original claims unless applied for within two years after the original patent grant.) The reissued patent will be good for the remaining unexpired portion of the original patent's term. 35 U.S.C.

§251. Other means of correcting mistakes in the original patent are described at 35 U.S.C. §§ 254-256.

*Assignments and Licenses*

A patent is a form of personal property and may be assigned, bequeathed by will, or pass to the owner's heirs through intestate succession. Applications for patent, issued patents, and interests in patents can be assigned through a written instrument. The P.T.O. records assignments sent to it for recording, and the recording serves as notice. An assignment will be void against a subsequent purchaser for valuable consideration without notice, unless it is recorded in the P.T.O. within three months of its date or prior to the date of the subsequent purchase. 35 U.S.C. § 261.

***Notes and Questions***

1. *The Patent Bar.* Any lawyer who is qualified to practice in the federal courts may represent clients in patent litigation. However, the PTO regulates who may represent clients in patent prosecutions. Both lawyers and non-lawyers may be eligible. To qualify, one must pass a rigorous written examination administered by the PTO, which tests knowledge of the substance and procedure of patent practice. To sit for this exam, one must generally demonstrate a substantial number of college course credits in engineering, a range of physical sciences, or computer science. Persons registered to practice before the PTO who are not lawyers are known as patent agents. Those who are lawyers are called patent attorneys. The specific requirements for PTO registration as a patent attorney are set forth at 37 C.F.R. §§ 11.5-11.8.

2. *Reexamination/Review.* Apart from the opportunity to make pre-issuance submissions, discussed *supra,* there is little opportunity for interested third parties who oppose the granting of a patent to influence the PTO's initial patentability decision. Generally such persons must wait and challenge the validity of the patent once it is issued. This may be done as a defense against a patent infringement claim or in a declaratory judgment action, if standing requirements are satisfied. For those wishing to avoid the burden of federal court

litigation, an administrative alternative is available pursuant to the reexamination provisions in Patent Act §§ 302-18.

Section 302 provides that any person may request that the validity of an issued patent claim be reexamined in light of prior art patents or printed publications. If the Commissioner of Patents determines that the request raises a substantial question of patentability that was not considered in the course of the patent application process, he must issue an order for reexamination to resolve the question. The reexamination is performed by a PTO examiner.

The patent owner may file a statement addressing the issues raised. She may propose amendments or new claims to distinguish her invention from the prior art (though she may not thus enlarge the scope of a disputed claim). The person requesting the reexamination may reply. Upon termination of the reexamination and any appeals by the patentee, the Commissioner will issue and publish a certificate canceling any claims determined to be unpatentable, confirming any claims determined to be patentable, and incorporating in the patent any proposed amended or new claims that have been determined to be patentable.

The Commissioner may commence a reexamination at his own initiative. Note also that the patentee may herself request a reexamination. Why might a patentee wish to do so?

How useful an alternative to litigation does the reexamination procedure described above provide to third parties wishing to challenge an issued patent? It has been suggested that the *ex parte* nature of the reexamination procedure, which limits the third party's opportunity to argue his position, discourages use of reexamination requests as an alternative to court challenges. See, e.g., Advisory Commission on Patent Law Reform, A Report to the Secretary of Commerce, 117-123 (1992).

In response to this criticism, in 1999, Congress enacted an alternative, or optional *inter partes* reexamination procedure, which is codified at Patent Act §§ 311-18. Under these provisions, as later amended, a third party requesting *inter partes* reexamination is entitled to receive a copy of all documents filed by the patentee and all communications from the PTO to the patentee during the course of the reexamination. Each time that the patentee files a response to an action on the merits from the PTO, the third-party requestor has the right to file written comments addressing the issues raised by the Office or the patentee's response. The requestor also may appeal a decision favorable to the patentee to the Board of Patent Appeals and Interferences, and subsequently to the Court of Appeals for the Federal Circuit. However, once the patentability issues raised by the third-party requestor have been resolved against the requestor under this procedure, he is estopped from raising them (or other issues that might have been raised in the reexamination) in a subsequent civil action.

This *inter partes* procedure has not proven to be as popular as was hoped. As the PTO has explained:

> Patentees insisted upon, and Congress legislated via the 1999 statute, that a challenger in an *inter partes* proceeding would be bound by its result by way of estoppel, including in subsequent litigation. However, the lack of such procedural mechanisms as discovery and cross-examination that would be available in litigation has apparently resulted in challengers being unwilling to invoke *inter partes* reexamination and risk its estoppel effect.

United States Patent and Trademark Office, *Report to Congress on Inter Partes Reexamination*, Executive Summary, *reprinted in* 69 Pat. Trademark & Copyright J. (B.N.A.) 204 (2004).

To further improve the administrative options for third parties to challenge patent validity, the America Invents Act § 6 replaces the existing "*inter partes* reexamination" with "*inter partes* review," and introduces a new "post-grant review" proceeding. Both proceedings are adjudicative patent revocation proceedings, rather than reexamination proceedings, and will be conducted by the Patent Trial and Appeal Board, rather than by an examiner. Both proceedings will provide opportunities for discovery, protective orders, and oral hearings, along with an opportunity for the patentee to amend or cancel claims. Pub. L. No. 112-29 § 6, 125 Stat. 299 (2011). The petitioner will only have to demonstrate patent invalidity by the preponderance of evidence (as contrasted to the "clear and convincing evidence" standard normally imposed on challenges to patent invalidity in litigation). Moreover, the new proceedings will move quickly--the Patent Trial and Appeals Board must reach a final determination within one year (with a possible 6-month extension for "good cause.") Either party may appeal the Board's decision on the merits to the Court of Appeals for the Federal Circuit. *Id.*

A post-grant review is only available in the case of patents filed on or after March 16, 2013. The petition for post-grant review must be instigated within the 9-month period immediately following grant of the patent. The challenger's petition for post-grant review may assert *any* ground for finding that the patent is invalid, including unpatentable subject matter and enablement (but not failure to satisfy the best mode requirement). Pub. L. No. 112-29 § 6(d), 125 Stat. 305 (2011) (amending 35 U.S.C. § 321)). The PTO Director must grant the petition if the information presented, if not rebutted, would demonstrate that "it is more likely than not that at least one of the claims challenged in the petition is unpatentable." Post-grant review may also be instituted if the petition raises "a novel or unsettled legal question that is important to other patents or patent applications." *Id.*, § 6(d) (amending 35 U.S.C. § 324)). Section 6 limits strategic use of post-grant reviews to harass patentees. For example, a petitioner who has already filed a declaratory judgment action for patent invalidity may not subsequently file for a post-grant review. If the petitioner commences a post-grant review and subsequently files for declaratory judgment, the declaratory judgment action must be stayed pending completion of the post-grant review, unless the patentee moves to lift the stay or files a civil action or counterclaim for infringement. (Note, however, that a petitioner may simultaneously pursue post-grant review and assert invalidity as a defense to an infringement claim in district court.) *Id.*, § 6(d)(amending 35 U.S.C. § 325)). Once the Patent Trial and Appeals Board issues a final written decision on the merits in a post-grant review proceeding, the petitioner is estopped from further challenging patentability in the PTO, the International Trade Commission and courts on any ground that was or reasonably could have been raised in the post-grant review proceeding. *Id.* Many other countries provide a similar form of administrative post-grant review for a short window of time after patent issuance. The AIA post-grant provision thus constitutes a further step towards harmonizing United States law with international patent norms.

The new *inter partes* review can only be instituted after the time to petition for post-grant review has passed (assuming that a post-grant review was available). If a post-grant review was instituted, the *inter partes* review can only be filed once the post-grant reveiw is completed. However, aside from these limitations, an *inter parties* review can be instituted at any time during the life of the patent. *Id.,* § 6(a) (amending 35 U.S.C.§ 311(c)). The grounds for challenge are more limited: a petition may only be based on prior art patents and printed publications, and challenge novelty or non-obviousness pursuant to Patent Act §§ 102 and 103. *Id.,* § 6(a) (amending 35 U.S.C. § 311(b)). In order to grant a petition for *inter partes* review, the Director must find that "there is a reasonable likelihood that the petitioner would prevail with respect to at least one of the claims challenged in the petition." *Id.,* § 6(a) (amending 35 U.S.C. §312(a)). This threshold standard is higher than under the old *inter partes* reexamination petition, where the Director needed only to find that the petition set forth a substantial new question of patentability. (The prior standard was considered to be too low, making it possible to use the reexamination procedure to harass patentees. According to report, 95% of petitions for *inter partes* reexamination were granted. H. Rep. No. 112-98, 112th Cong., 1st Sess. Part 1, 47 (2011)). The same rules prohibiting simultaneous administrative review and declaratory judgment actions apply as in the case of post-grant review. In addition, a third party may not petition for *inter partes* review more than a year after being served with a complaint for infringement. *Id.,* §6(a) (amending 35 U.S.C. § 315(a)-(b)). The same rules regarding estopple apply as in the case of post-grant review, as well. *Id.* (amending 35 U.S.C. § 315(e)). The new *inter partes* review proceeding became available and replaced *inter partes* reexamination on September 16, 2012. It is now applicable to all patents, regardless of when they were filed. *Id.,* § 6(c).

Why not permit challenges to validity on all grounds, throughout the life of the patent? In your opinion, will the America

Invents Act's precautions to prevent use of administrative proceedings to harass patentees be sufficient? Are the new proceedings likely to undermine the value of patents, as some critics have claimed? Are they likely to have disparate impact? Some critics have argued that to take advantage of the new post-grant review, patentees must closely monitor the actions of the PTO. Since only big businesses have the resources to monitor the issuance of new patents, they will be the only ones to benefit.

3. *The Patent Term.* Review the language of Patent Act § 154. The United States had for many years granted a term of 17 years for utility patents, measured from the date the patent issued. In 1994, Congress amended §154 to substitute a term of 20 years, measured from the earliest U.S. patent application filing date. The United States' acceptance of the TRIPs Agreement necessitated the change. There was significant resistance to measuring the patent term from the application date due to fear that this would decrease the term whenever the application process took over 3 years. To ensure equitable treatment, the amendment provided for restoration of time lost from delays attributable to national security concerns, interference proceedings, or successful appeals of PTO decisions, as described below. The new term was effective for patents granted on applications filed after June 8, 1995. Under a transition provision, patents in existence on June 8, 1995 or granted on applications filed prior to that date will endure for the longer of 17 years from issuance or 20 years from application date. See 35 U.S.C.A. §154(c).

As noted above, when it changed the means of measuring the patent term, Congress undertook to guarantee that patentees would enjoy *at least* 17 years of protection under the 20-years-from-filing term measure. Congress provided (subject to certain exceptions and limitations) that the PTO *must* grant a patent within three years of the patent's U.S. filing date. For each day the PTO delays beyond the three-year period, a day will be added to the end of the patentee's term. However, the additional period will be reduced by any period of time in which the patentee failed to engage in reasonable efforts to conclude prosecution. This is to prevent patent applicants from using the term guarantee provisions strategically. See 35 U.S.C.A. § 154(b).

Even though the TRIPs amendments *measure* the patent term from the patent application date, patent protection *commences* upon patent issuance, as was the case prior to the amendments. In 1999, Congress further amended the Patent Act to provide that most patent applications would be published 18 months after their earliest filing date, and that patentees would enjoy limited, "provisional" rights against infringement during the period between publication and issuance. See 35 U.S.C. §154(d). These provisional rights will be discussed more fully *infra.*

# E. THE PATENTEE'S RIGHTS

## 1. The Right To Exclude Others from Directly Infringing the Patent

*Page 274: Add the following discussion to the end of Note 2:*

In Transocean Offshore Deepwater Drilling, Inc. v. Maersk Contractors U.S.A., Inc., 617 F.3d 1296, 1296 (Fed. Cir. 2010), two U.S. companies negotiated and signed a contract in Norway for sale of an allegedly infringing drilling rig to be used in the United States. The issue was whether this constituted either an infringing offer to sell or an infringing sale. The Federal Circuit found that it could constitute both. The court first explained that an offer to sell differs from a sale, for purposes of Patent Act § 271(a), because an offer to sell need not be accepted to constitute an act of infringement. The court noted that offers to sell should be analyzed using traditional contract principles. *Id.,* at 1308. In *Transocean,* there was no dispute that an offer to sell had been made. However, the defendant argued (and the district court had agreed), that there could be no finding of infringement because the alleged offer and sale had occurred abroad. The Federal Circuit disagreed, explaining:

> This case presents the question whether an offer which is made in Norway by a U.S. company to a U.S. company to

sell a product within the U.S., for delivery and use within the U.S. constitutes an offer to sell within the U.S. under § 271(a). We conclude that it does. Section 271(a) states that "whoever ... offers to sell ... within the United States any patented invention ... infringes." In order for an offer to sell to constitute infringement, the offer must be to sell a patented invention within the United States. The focus should not be on the location of the offer, but rather the location of the future sale that would occur pursuant to the offer.

The offer to sell liability was added to the patent statute to conform to the April 1994 Uruguay Round's Trade-Related Aspects of Intellectual Property Agreement (TRIPS). The underlying purpose of holding someone who offers to sell liable for infringement is to prevent "generating interest in a potential infringing product to the commercial detriment of the rightful patentee." The offer must be for a potentially infringing article. We are mindful of the presumption against extraterritoriality. "It is the general rule under United States patent law that no infringement occurs when a patented product is made and sold in another country." This presumption has guided other courts to conclude that the contemplated sale [must] occur within the United States in order for an offer to sell to constitute infringement. We agree that the location of the contemplated sale controls whether there is an offer to sell within the United States.

The statute precludes "offers to sell ... within the United States." To adopt Maersk USA's position would have us read the statute as "offers made within the United States to sell" or "offers made within the United States to sell within the United States." First, this is not the statutory language. Second, this interpretation would exalt form over substance by allowing a U.S. company to travel abroad to make offers to sell back into the U.S. without any liability for infringement. * * * These acts create a real harm in the U.S. to a U.S. patentee.

* * *

> * * * The fact that the offer was negotiated or a contract signed while the two U.S. companies were abroad does not remove this case from statutory liability. We therefore vacate the district court's summary judgment of non-infringement.

617 F.3d at 309-10. In a footnote, the court further explained that to determine whether an offer was to sell "the patented invention," the court must consider "what was offered for sale, not what was ultimately delivered." Thus, it did not matter in *Transocean* that the seller eventually altered the drill rig design prior to delivery, since the subject of the offer to sell was the unmodified rig. *Id.*, at 310 n. 4. Under the court's reasoning, would there be infringement if the offering party was not a U.S. company?

The court then turned to the question of whether there could also be an infringing "sale" under the facts before it:

> As with the offer to sell, we hold that a contract between two U.S. companies for the sale of the patented invention with delivery and performance in the U.S. constitutes a sale under § 271(a) as a matter of law. Maersk USA's first argument, that the location of negotiation and contracting should control is contrary to our precedent in *Litecubes.* There, we held that a sale does not only occur at a "single point where some legally operative act took place." *Litecubes,* 523 F.3d at 1369-70. We may also consider other factors such as the place of performance. Maersk USA's argument that Statoil could use the rig outside the U.S. ignores the plain language of the contract, which includes an "Operating Area" of the U.S. Gulf of Mexico. It also ignores the fact that Maersk did in fact deliver the rig to U.S. waters. Maersk USA's remaining arguments regarding the right to alter the final design and the fact that the rig was not complete at the time of contracting do not change the result. Maersk USA and Statoil signed a contract and the schematics that accompanied that contract could support a finding that the sale was of an infringing article under § 271(a). The fact that Maersk USA, after the execution of the contract, altered the rig in response to the GSF injunction is irrelevant to this infringement analysis. The potentially

> infringing article is the rig sold in the contract, not the altered rig that Maersk USA delivered to the U.S.
>
> Finally, we reject Maersk USA's claim that the entire apparatus must have been constructed and ready for use in order to have been sold. Our precedent establishes that a contract can constitute a sale to trigger infringement liability. *See NTP, Inc. v. Research in Motion, Ltd.*, 418 F.3d 1282, 1319 (Fed.Cir.2005). A "sale" is not limited to the transfer of tangible property; a sale may also be the agreement by which such a transfer takes place. In this case, there was a contract to sell a rig that included schematics. On summary judgment, we must draw all justifiable inferences in favor of the nonmovant, Transocean. Transocean argues that these schematics show sale of the patented invention. This is a genuine issue of material fact sufficient to withstand summary judgment.

*Id.*, at 311. Can the Federal Circuit's decision be reconciled with the Supreme Court's decision in *Deepsouth?*

*Page 295: Renumber Note 4 Experimental Use as Note 5, and add the following new Note 4:*

4. *Self-replicating technologies.* Monsanto Company genetically engineered and patented "Roundup Ready" soybeans. When planted, the genetically engineered beans (which are seeds) grow into plants that survive exposure to an important herbicide used by farmers to control weeds. The Monsanto beans/seeds pass this patented herbicide-resistant trait from one generation to the next. The patentee sells the beans/seeds subject to a licensing agreement that permits farmers to plant the purchased beans in only one growing season. Farmers may consume or sell the resulting soy bean crops for consumption, but are expressly denied permission to replant any of the harvested soybeans. Some farmers who grow the patented soybeans sell them to a grain elevator. Farmer Bowman purchases those beans from the grain elevator and plants them. He then harvests the crop, saves some of the beans/seeds, and replants them in subsequent years.

Monsanto sues Bowman for patent infringement. Is Bowman protected by the doctrine of patent exhaustion? Why or why not?

In *Bowman v. Monsanto Co.,* __ U.S. __, 133 S.Ct. 1761, (2013), the Supreme Court unanimously ruled that the doctrine of exhaustion did not apply:

> Under the patent exhaustion doctrine, Bowman could resell the patented soybeans he purchased from the grain elevator; so too he could consume the beans himself or feed them to his animals. Monsanto, although the patent holder, would have no business interfering in those uses of Roundup Ready beans. But the exhaustion doctrine does not enable Bowman to make *additional* patented soybeans without Monsanto's permission (either express or implied). And that is precisely what Bowman did.

*Id.,* 133 S.Ct. at 1766. What are the implications of this decision for farmers and their traditional ways of conducting business? What are the implications of the decision for other "self-replicating" technologies, such as man-made cell lines, DNA molecules, and nanotechnology? Can you think of potential problems? Justice Kagan, writing for the Court, made a point of limiting the holding to the specific situation before the Court:

> We realize that [self-replicating] inventions are becoming ever more prevalent, complex, and diverse. In another case, the article's self-replication might occur outside the purchaser's control. Or it might be a necessary but incidental step in using the item for another purpose. * * * We need not address here whether or how the doctrine of patent exhaustion would apply in such circumstances.

*Id.,* at 1769.

## 2. The Right to Exclude Others From Assisting Third Parties to Infringe

*Page 307: Add the following case decision, directly following the DSU decision, and before the Notes and Questions:*

## Global-Tech Appliances, Inc. v. SEB S.A.

United States Supreme Court, 2011.
__ U.S. __, 131 S.Ct. 2060, 179 L.Ed.2d 1167.

Justice ALITO delivered the opinion of the Court.

We consider whether a party who "actively induces infringement of a patent" under 35 U.S.C. § 271(b) must know that the induced acts constitute patent infringement.

I

This case concerns a patent for an innovative deep fryer designed by respondent SEB S.A., a French maker of home appliances. In the late 1980's, SEB invented a "cool-touch" deep fryer, that is, a deep fryer for home use with external surfaces that remain cool during the frying process. The cool-touch deep fryer consisted of a metal frying pot surrounded by a plastic outer housing. Attached to the housing was a ring that suspended the metal pot and insulated the housing from heat by separating it from the pot, creating air space between the two components. SEB obtained a U.S. patent for its design in 1991, and sometime later, SEB started manufacturing the cool-touch fryer and selling it in this country under its well-known "T–Fal" brand. Superior to other products in the American market at the time, SEB's fryer was a commercial success.

In 1997, Sunbeam Products, Inc., a U.S. competitor of SEB, asked petitioner Pentalpha Enterprises, Ltd., to supply it with deep fryers meeting certain specifications. Pentalpha is a Hong Kong maker of home appliances and a wholly owned subsidiary of petitioner Global–Tech Appliances, Inc.[1]

---

[1] We refer to both petitioners as "Pentalpha."

In order to develop a deep fryer for Sunbeam, Pentalpha purchased an SEB fryer in Hong Kong and copied all but its cosmetic features. Because the SEB fryer bought in Hong Kong was made for sale in a foreign market, it bore no U.S. patent markings. After copying SEB's design, Pentalpha retained an attorney to conduct a right-to-use study, but Pentalpha refrained from telling the attorney that its design was copied directly from SEB's.

The attorney failed to locate SEB's patent, and in August 1997 he issued an opinion letter stating that Pentalpha's deep fryer did not infringe any of the patents that he had found. That same month, Pentalpha started selling its deep fryers to Sunbeam, which resold them in the United States under its trademarks. By obtaining its product from a manufacturer with lower production costs, Sunbeam was able to undercut SEB in the U.S. market.

After SEB's customers started defecting to Sunbeam, SEB sued Sunbeam in March 1998, alleging that Sunbeam's sales infringed SEB's patent. Sunbeam notified Pentalpha of the lawsuit the following month. Undeterred, Pentalpha went on to sell deep fryers to Fingerhut Corp. and Montgomery Ward & Co., both of which resold them in the United States under their respective trademarks.

SEB settled the lawsuit with Sunbeam, and then sued Pentalpha, asserting two theories of recovery: First, SEB claimed that Pentalpha had directly infringed SEB's patent in violation of 35 U.S.C. § 271(a), by selling or offering to sell its deep fryers; and second, SEB claimed that Pentalpha had contravened § 271(b) by actively inducing Sunbeam, Fingerhut, and Montgomery Ward to sell or to offer to sell Pentalpha's deep fryers in violation of SEB's patent rights.

Following a 5–day trial, the jury found for SEB on both theories and also found that Pentalpha's infringement had been willful. Pentalpha filed post-trial motions seeking a new trial or judgment as a matter of law on several grounds. As relevant here, Pentalpha argued that there was insufficient evidence to support the jury's finding of induced infringement under § 271(b) because Pentalpha did not actually know of SEB's patent until it received the notice of the Sunbeam lawsuit in April 1998.

The District Court rejected Pentalpha's argument, as did the Court of Appeals for the Federal Circuit, which affirmed the judgment. Summarizing a recent en banc decision, the Federal Circuit stated that induced infringement under § 271(b) requires a "plaintiff [to] show that the alleged infringer knew or should have known that his actions would induce actual infringements" and that this showing includes proof that the alleged infringer knew of the patent. Although the record contained no direct evidence that Pentalpha knew of SEB's patent before April 1998, the court found adequate evidence to support a finding that "Pentalpha deliberately disregarded a known risk that SEB had a protective patent." Such disregard, the court said, "is not different from actual knowledge, but is a form of actual knowledge."

* * *

II

Pentalpha argues that active inducement liability under § 271(b) requires more than deliberate indifference to a known risk that the induced acts may violate an existing patent. Instead, Pentalpha maintains, actual knowledge of the patent is needed.

A

In assessing Pentalpha's argument, we begin with the text of § 271(b)—which is short, simple, and, with respect to the question presented in this case, inconclusive. Section 271(b) states: "Whoever actively induces infringement of a patent shall be liable as an infringer."

Although the text of § 271(b) makes no mention of intent, we infer that at least some intent is required. The term "induce" means "[t]o lead on; to influence; to prevail on; to move by persuasion or influence." Webster's New International Dictionary 1269 (2d ed.1945). The addition of the adverb "actively" suggests that the inducement must involve the taking of affirmative steps to bring about the desired result.

When a person actively induces another to take some action, the inducer obviously knows the action that he or she wishes to bring about. If a used car salesman induces a customer to buy a car, the salesman knows that the desired result is the purchase of the car. But what if it is said that the salesman induced the customer to buy a *damaged* car? Does this mean merely that the salesman induced the customer to purchase a car that happened to be damaged, a fact of which the salesman may have been unaware? Or does this mean that the salesman knew that the car was damaged? The statement that the salesman induced the customer to buy a damaged car is ambiguous.

So is § 271(b). In referring to a party that "induces infringement," this provision may require merely that the inducer lead another to engage in conduct that happens to amount to infringement, *i.e.,* the making, using, offering to sell, selling, or importing of a patented invention. On the other hand, the reference to a party that "induces infringement" may also be read to mean that the inducer must persuade another to engage in conduct that the inducer knows is infringement. Both readings are possible.

B

Finding no definitive answer in the statutory text, we turn to the case law that predates the enactment of § 271 as part the Patent Act of 1952. As we recognized in *Aro Mfg. Co. v. Convertible Top Replacement Co.,* 377 U.S. 476 (1964) *(Aro II),* "[t]he section was designed to 'codify in statutory form principles of contributory infringement' which had been 'part of our law for about 80 years.' " *Id.*, at 485–486.

Unfortunately, the relevant pre–1952 cases are less clear than one might hope with respect to the question presented here. Before 1952, both the conduct now covered by § 271(b) (induced infringement) and the conduct now addressed by § 271(c) (sale of a component of a patented invention) were viewed as falling within the overarching concept of "contributory infringement." Cases in the latter category—*i.e.,* cases in which a party sold an item that was not itself covered by the claims of a patent but that enabled another party to make or use a patented machine, process, or combination—were more common.

The pre–1952 case law provides conflicting signals regarding the intent needed in such cases. In an oft-cited decision, then-Judge

Taft suggested that it was sufficient if the seller of the component part intended that the part be used in an invention that happened to infringe a patent. He wrote that it was "well settled that where one makes and sells one element of a combination covered by a patent with the intention and for the purpose of bringing about its use in such a combination he is guilty of contributory infringement." *Thomson–Houston Elec. Co. v. Ohio Brass Co.,* 80 F. 712, 721 (C.A.6 1897).

On the other hand, this Court, in *Henry v. A.B. Dick Co.,* 224 U.S. 1 (1912), overruled on other grounds, *Motion Picture Patents Co. v. Universal Film Mfg. Co.,* 243 U.S. 502 (1917), stated that "if the defendants [who were accused of contributory infringement] *knew of the patent* and that [the direct infringer] had unlawfully made the patented article ... with the intent and purpose that [the direct infringer] should use the infringing article ... they would assist in her infringing use." 224 U.S., at 33 (emphasis added and deleted). Our decision in *Metro–Goldwyn–Mayer Studios Inc. v. Grokster, Ltd.,* 545 U.S. 913 (2005), which looked to the law of contributory patent infringement for guidance in determining the standard to be applied in a case claiming contributory copyright infringement, contains dicta that may be read as interpreting the pre–1952 cases this way. In *Grokster,* we said that "[t]he inducement rule ... premises liability on purposeful, culpable expression and conduct." *Id.*, at 937.

While both the language of § 271(b) and the pre–1952 case law that this provision was meant to codify are susceptible to conflicting interpretations, our decision in *Aro II* resolves the question in this case. In *Aro II,* a majority held that a violator of § 271(c) must know "that the combination for which his component was especially designed was both patented and infringing," and as we explain below, that conclusion compels this same knowledge for liability under § 271(b).

C

As noted above, induced infringement was not considered a separate theory of indirect liability in the pre–1952 case law. Rather, it was treated as evidence of "contributory infringement," that is, the aiding and abetting of direct infringement by another party. When Congress enacted § 271, it separated what had previously been regarded as contributory infringement into two categories, one covered by § 271(b) and the other covered by § 271(c).

*Aro II* concerned § 271(c), which states in relevant part:

> "Whoever offers to sell or sells ... a component of a patented [invention] ..., constituting a material part of the invention, *knowing the same to be especially made or especially adapted for use in an infringement* of such patent, and not a staple article or commodity of commerce suitable for substantial noninfringing use, shall be liable as a contributory infringer." (Emphasis added.)

This language contains exactly the same ambiguity as § 271(b). The phrase "knowing [a component] to be especially made or especially adapted for use in an infringement" may be read to mean that a violator must know that the component is "especially adapted for use" in a product that happens to infringe a patent. Or the phrase may be read to require, in addition, knowledge of the patent's existence.

This question closely divided the *Aro II* Court. In a badly fractured decision, a majority concluded that knowledge of the patent was needed. Justice Black's opinion, which explained the basis for the majority's view, concluded that the language of § 271(c) supported this interpretation. His opinion also relied on an amendment to this language that was adopted when the bill was in committee.

Four Justices disagreed with this interpretation and would have held that a violator of § 271(c) need know only that the component is specially adapted for use in a product that happens to infringe a patent. These Justices thought that this reading was supported by the language of § 271(c) and the pre–1952 case law, and they disagreed with the inference drawn by the majority from the amendment of § 271(c)'s language.

While there is much to be said in favor of both views expressed in *Aro II,* the "holding in *Aro II* has become a fixture in the law of contributory infringement under [section] 271(c)"—so much so that SEB has not asked us to overrule it. Nor has Congress seen fit to alter

§ 271(c)'s intent requirement in the nearly half a century since *Aro II* was decided. In light of the " 'special force' " of the doctrine of *stare decisis* with regard to questions of statutory interpretation, we proceed on the premise that § 271(c) requires knowledge of the existence of the patent that is infringed.

Based on this premise, it follows that the same knowledge is needed for induced infringement under § 271(b). As noted, the two provisions have a common origin in the pre–1952 understanding of contributory infringement, and the language of the two provisions creates the same difficult interpretive choice. It would thus be strange to hold that knowledge of the relevant patent is needed under § 271(c) but not under § 271(b).

Accordingly, we now hold that induced infringement under § 271(b) requires knowledge that the induced acts constitute patent infringement.

III

Returning to Pentalpha's principal challenge, we agree that deliberate indifference to a known risk that a patent exists is not the appropriate standard under § 271(b). We nevertheless affirm the judgment of the Court of Appeals because the evidence in this case was plainly sufficient to support a finding of Pentalpha's knowledge under the doctrine of willful blindness.

A

The doctrine of willful blindness is well established in criminal law. Many criminal statutes require proof that a defendant acted knowingly or willfully, and courts applying the doctrine of willful blindness hold that defendants cannot escape the reach of these statutes by deliberately shielding themselves from clear evidence of critical facts that are strongly suggested by the circumstances. The traditional rationale for this doctrine is that defendants who behave in this manner are just as culpable as those who have actual knowledge. * * * It is also said that persons who know enough to blind themselves to direct proof of critical facts in effect have actual knowledge of those facts.

This Court's opinion more than a century ago in *Spurr v. United States,* 174 U.S. 728 (1899), while not using the term "willful blindness," endorsed a similar concept. The case involved a criminal statute that prohibited a bank officer from "willfully" certifying a check drawn against insufficient funds. We said that a willful violation would occur "if the [bank] officer purposely keeps himself in ignorance of whether the drawer has money in the bank." Following our decision in *Spurr,* several federal prosecutions in the first half of the 20th century invoked the doctrine of willful blindness. Later, a 1962 proposed draft of the Model Penal Code, which has since become official, attempted to incorporate the doctrine by defining "knowledge of the existence of a particular fact" to include a situation in which "a person is aware of a high probability of [the fact's] existence, unless he actually believes that it does not exist." ALI, Model Penal Code § 2.02(7) (Proposed Official Draft 1962). Our Court has used the Code's definition as a guide in analyzing whether certain statutory presumptions of knowledge comported with due process. And every Court of Appeals—with the possible exception of the District of Columbia Circuit—has fully embraced willful blindness, applying the doctrine to a wide range of criminal statutes.

Given the long history of willful blindness and its wide acceptance in the Federal Judiciary, we can see no reason why the doctrine should not apply in civil lawsuits for induced patent infringement under 35 U.S.C. § 271(b).

Pentalpha urges us not to take this step, arguing that § 271(b) demands more than willful blindness with respect to *the induced acts* that constitute infringement. This question, however, is not at issue here. There is no need to invoke the doctrine of willful blindness to establish that Pentalpha knew that the retailers who purchased its fryer were selling that product in the American market; Pentalpha was indisputably aware that its customers were selling its product in this country.

* * *

B

While the Courts of Appeals articulate the doctrine of willful blindness in slightly different ways, all appear to agree on two basic requirements: (1) the defendant must subjectively believe that there is a high probability that a fact exists and (2) the defendant must take deliberate actions to avoid learning of that fact. We think these requirements give willful blindness an appropriately limited scope that surpasses recklessness and negligence. Under this formulation, a willfully blind defendant is one who takes deliberate actions to avoid confirming a high probability of wrongdoing and who can almost be said to have actually known the critical facts. * * * By contrast, a reckless defendant is one who merely knows of a substantial and unjustified risk of such wrongdoing, and a negligent defendant is one who should have known of a similar risk but, in fact, did not.

The test applied by the Federal Circuit in this case departs from the proper willful blindness standard in two important respects. First, it permits a finding of knowledge when there is merely a "known risk" that the induced acts are infringing. Second, in demanding only "deliberate indifference" to that risk, the Federal Circuit's test does not require active efforts by an inducer to avoid knowing about the infringing nature of the activities.

In spite of these flaws, we believe that the evidence when viewed in the light most favorable to the verdict for SEB is sufficient under the correct standard. The jury could have easily found that before April 1998 Pentalpha willfully blinded itself to the infringing nature of the sales it encouraged Sunbeam to make.

SEB's cool-touch fryer was an innovation in the U.S. market when Pentalpha copied it. As one would expect with any superior product, sales of SEB's fryer had been growing for some time. Pentalpha knew all of this, for its CEO and president, John Sham, testified that, in developing a product for Sunbeam, Pentalpha performed "market research" and "gather[ed] information as much as possible." Pentalpha's belief that SEB's fryer embodied advanced technology that would be valuable in the U.S. market is evidenced by its decision to copy all but the cosmetic features of SEB's fryer.

Also revealing is Pentalpha's decision to copy an overseas model of SEB's fryer. Pentalpha knew that the product it was designing was for the U.S. market, and Sham—himself a named inventor on numerous U.S. patents—was well aware that products made for overseas markets usually do not bear U.S. patent markings. Even more telling is Sham's decision not to inform the attorney from whom Pentalpha sought a right-to-use opinion that the product to be evaluated was simply a knockoff of SEB's deep fryer. On the facts of this case, we cannot fathom what motive Sham could have had for withholding this information other than to manufacture a claim of plausible deniability in the event that his company was later accused of patent infringement. Nor does Sham's testimony on this subject provide any reason to doubt that inference. Asked whether the attorney would have fared better had he known of SEB's design, Sham was nonresponsive. All he could say was that a patent search is not an "easy job" and that is why he hired attorneys to perform them.

Taken together, this evidence was more than sufficient for a jury to find that Pentalpha subjectively believed there was a high probability that SEB's fryer was patented, that Pentalpha took deliberate steps to avoid knowing that fact, and that it therefore willfully blinded itself to the infringing nature of Sunbeam's sales.

* * *

*Page 309, Note 2: Replace the first paragraph with the following:*

2. *Active inducement to infringe.* Under § 271(b), a person who actively solicits or assists direct infringement with the requisite intent will be liable if his actions in fact result in patent infringement. What kinds of acts might constitute active inducement? Is there any overlap between subsections (b) and (c), so that a defendant's conduct might simultaneously violate both? Why is the active inducement cause of action needed?

What kind of evidence might be used to demonstrate the necessary intent and knowledge or "willful blindness" to constitute inducement? In the past, courts have often looked to whether the defendant consulted with qualified counsel and reasonably relied upon the lawyer's advice. However, the America Invents Act § 17 adds a new Patent Act § 298, which provides:

> The failure of an infringer to obtain the advice of counsel with respect to any allegedly infringed patent, or the failure of the infringer to present such advice to the court or jury, may not be used to prove that the accused infringer willfully infringed the patent or that the infringer intended to induce infringement of the patent.

Pub. L. No. 112-29 § 17, 125 Stat. 329 (2011). Why might Congress have deemed this prohibition desirable?

What does it take to demonstrate that the defendant's acts have induced direct infringement? In Akamai Technologies, Inc. v. Limelight Networks, Inc., 692 F.3d 1301 (Fed. Cir. 2012) (*en banc*), the Federal Circuit, sitting *en banc*, held that the act of direct infringement necessary for purposes of an inducement claim need not be an act that would result in *direct infringement liability.* Rather, while all the steps of a patented method must be performed in order to find induced infringement, it is *not necessary to prove that all the steps were committed by a single entity:*

> Requiring proof that there *has been* direct infringement as a predicate for induced infringement is not the same as requiring proof that a single party would be *liable* as a direct infringer. If a party has knowingly induced others to commit the acts necessary to infringe the plaintiff's patent and those others commit those acts, there is no reason to immunize the inducer from liability for indirect infringement simply because the parties have structured their conduct so that no single defendant has committed all the acts necessary to give rise to liability for direct infringement.
>
> A party who knowingly induces others to engage in acts that collectively practice the steps of the patented method—and those others perform those acts—has had precisely the same impact on the patentee as a party who induces the same infringement by a single direct infringer; there is no reason, either in the text of the statute or in the policy underlying it, to

> treat the two inducers differently. In particular, there is no reason to hold that the second inducer is liable for infringement but the first is not.
>
> Likewise, a party who performs some of the steps itself and induces another to perform the remaining steps that constitute infringement has precisely the same impact on the patentee as a party who induces a single person to carry out all of the steps. It would be a bizarre result to hold someone liable for inducing another to perform all of the steps of a method claim but to hold harmless one who goes further by actually performing some of the steps himself. The party who actually participates in performing the infringing method is, if anything, more culpable than one who does not perform any steps.

*Id.,* 692 F.3d at 308-09 (emphasis in original). Did the court define "direct infringement" to mean different things in the context of § 102(b) and 102(a)? The majority rejected this criticism:

> Judge Linn's dissent argues that the approach we adopt today has the effect of "defin[ing] direct infringement differently for the purposes of establishing liability under § 271(a) and (b)." That is not so, and the structure of section 271 explains why. Section 271(a) does not define the term "infringement." Instead, it simply sets forth a type of conduct that qualifies as infringing, i.e., it provides that anyone who makes, uses, or sells, etc., any patented invention "infringes the patent." Section 271(b) sets forth another type of conduct that qualifies as infringing, i.e., it provides that anyone who induces infringement "shall be liable as an infringer." But nothing in the text of either subsection suggests that the act of "infringement" required for inducement under section 271(b) must qualify as an act that would make a person liable as an infringer under section 271(a).

*Id.,* at 1314.

## G. DEFENSES AND REMEDIES

## 1. Defenses

* * *

### b. Inequitable Conduct

*Pages 340-341: Replace the text of subsection b. Inequitable Conduct with the following:*

The judge-made inequitable conduct defense holds that if the patentee intentionally misrepresented or withheld material information concerning the patentability of the invention from the PTO in the course of prosecution, the patent will not be enforced. In Therasense, Inc. v. Becton, Dickinson & Co., 649 F.3d 1276 (Fed. Cir. 2011), the Court of Appeals for the Federal Circuit, sitting *en banc*, recently discussed the origin and purpose of the inequitable conduct defense and the problems that have arisen in applying it. The court undertook to establish unified standards for applying it:

> To prevail on the defense of inequitable conduct, the accused infringer must prove that the applicant misrepresented or omitted material information with the specific intent to deceive the PTO. The accused infringer must prove both elements—intent and materiality—by clear and convincing evidence. If the accused infringer meets its burden, then the district court must weigh the equities to determine whether the applicant's conduct before the PTO warrants rendering the entire patent unenforceable.
>
> * * *
>
> [T]he standards for intent to deceive and materiality have fluctuated over time. In the past, this court has espoused low standards for meeting the intent requirement, finding it satisfied based on gross negligence or even negligence. * * * This court has also previously adopted a broad view of materiality, using a "reasonable examiner" standard based on the PTO's 1977 amendment to Rule 56. * * * 37 C.F.R. § 1.56

(1977) (a reference is material if "there is a substantial likelihood that a reasonable examiner would consider it important in deciding whether to allow the application to issue as a patent"). Further weakening the showing needed to establish inequitable conduct, this court then placed intent and materiality together on a "sliding scale." This modification to the inequitable conduct doctrine held patents unenforceable based on a reduced showing of intent if the record contained a strong showing of materiality, and vice versa. In effect, this change conflated, and diluted, the standards for both intent and materiality.

This court embraced these reduced standards for intent and materiality to foster full disclosure to the PTO. This new focus on encouraging disclosure has had numerous unforeseen and unintended consequences. Most prominently, inequitable conduct has become a significant litigation strategy. A charge of inequitable conduct conveniently expands discovery into corporate practices before patent filing and disqualifies the prosecuting attorney from the patentee's litigation team. Moreover, inequitable conduct charges cast a dark cloud over the patent's validity and paint the patentee as a bad actor. Because the doctrine focuses on the moral turpitude of the patentee with ruinous consequences for the reputation of his patent attorney, it discourages settlement and deflects attention from the merits of validity and infringement issues. Inequitable conduct disputes also "increas[e] the complexity, duration and cost of patent infringement litigation that is already notorious for its complexity and high cost."

Perhaps most importantly, the remedy for inequitable conduct is the "atomic bomb" of patent law. Unlike validity defenses, which are claim specific, inequitable conduct regarding any single claim renders the entire patent unenforceable. Unlike other deficiencies, inequitable conduct cannot be cured by reissue. Moreover, the taint of a finding of inequitable conduct can spread from a single patent to render unenforceable other related patents and applications in the same technology family. Thus, a finding of inequitable conduct may endanger a substantial portion of a company's patent portfolio.

A finding of inequitable conduct may also spawn antitrust and unfair competition claims. Further, prevailing on a claim of inequitable conduct often makes a case "exceptional," leading potentially to an award of attorneys' fees under 35 U.S.C. § 285. A finding of inequitable conduct may also prove the crime or fraud exception to the attorney-client privilege.

With these far-reaching consequences, it is no wonder that charging inequitable conduct has become a common litigation tactic. One study estimated that eighty percent of patent infringement cases included allegations of inequitable conduct. Inequitable conduct "has been overplayed, is appearing in nearly every patent suit, and is cluttering up the patent system." "[T]he habit of charging inequitable conduct in almost every major patent case has become an absolute plague. Reputable lawyers seem to feel compelled to make the charge against other reputable lawyers on the slenderest grounds, to represent their client's interests adequately, perhaps."

Left unfettered, the inequitable conduct doctrine has plagued not only the courts but also the entire patent system. Because allegations of inequitable conduct are routinely brought on "the slenderest grounds," patent prosecutors constantly confront the specter of inequitable conduct charges. With inequitable conduct casting the shadow of a hangman's noose, it is unsurprising that patent prosecutors regularly bury PTO examiners with a deluge of prior art references, most of which have marginal value. * * * "Applicants disclose too much prior art for the PTO to meaningfully consider, and do not explain its significance, all out of fear that to do otherwise risks a claim of inequitable conduct." This tidal wave of disclosure makes identifying the most relevant prior art more difficult. * * * "This flood of information strains the agency's examining resources and directly contributes to the backlog."

While honesty at the PTO is essential, low standards for intent and materiality have inadvertently led to many unintended consequences, among them, increased adjudication cost and complexity, reduced likelihood of settlement, burdened courts, strained PTO resources, increased PTO backlog, and impaired patent quality. This court now tightens the standards for finding both intent and materiality in order to redirect a doctrine that has been overused to the detriment of the public.

* * *

To prevail on a claim of inequitable conduct, the accused infringer must prove that the patentee acted with the specific intent to deceive the PTO. A finding that the misrepresentation or omission amounts to gross negligence or negligence under a "should have known" standard does not satisfy this intent requirement. "In a case involving nondisclosure of information, clear and convincing evidence must show that the applicant *made a deliberate decision* to withhold a *known* material reference." In other words, the accused infringer must prove by clear and convincing evidence that the applicant knew of the reference, knew that it was material, and made a deliberate decision to withhold it.

* * *

Intent and materiality are separate requirements. A district court should not use a "sliding scale," where a weak showing of intent may be found sufficient based on a strong showing of materiality, and vice versa. Moreover, a district court may not infer intent solely from materiality. Instead, a court must weigh the evidence of intent to deceive independent of its analysis of materiality. Proving that the applicant knew of a reference, should have known of its materiality, and decided not to submit it to the PTO does not prove specific intent to deceive. * * *

Because direct evidence of deceptive intent is rare, a district court may infer intent from indirect and circumstantial evidence. However, to meet the clear and convincing evidence standard, the specific intent to deceive must be "the single most reasonable inference able to be drawn from the evidence." Indeed, the evidence "must be sufficient to *require* a finding of deceitful intent in the light of all the circumstances." Hence, when there are multiple reasonable inferences that may be drawn, intent to deceive cannot be found. * * * This court reviews the district court's factual findings regarding what reasonable inferences may be drawn from the evidence for clear error.

Because the party alleging inequitable conduct bears the burden of proof, the "patentee need not offer any good faith explanation unless the accused infringer first ... prove[s] a threshold level of intent to deceive by clear and convincing evidence." The absence of a good faith explanation for withholding a material reference does not, by itself, prove intent to deceive.

* * *

This court holds that, as a general matter, the materiality required to establish inequitable conduct is but-for materiality. When an applicant fails to disclose prior art to the PTO, that prior art is but-for material if the PTO would not have allowed a claim had it been aware of the undisclosed prior art. Hence, in assessing the materiality of a withheld reference, the court must determine whether the PTO would have allowed the claim if it had been aware of the undisclosed reference. In making this patentability determination, the court should apply the preponderance of the evidence standard and give claims their broadest reasonable construction. Often the patentability of a claim will be congruent with the validity determination—if a claim is properly invalidated in district court based on the deliberately withheld reference, then that reference is necessarily material because a finding of invalidity in a district court requires clear and convincing evidence, a higher evidentiary burden than that used in prosecution at the PTO. However, even if a district court does not invalidate a claim based on a deliberately withheld reference, the reference may be material if it would have blocked patent issuance under the

PTO's different evidentiary standards. *See* MPEP §§ 706 (preponderance of the evidence), 2111 (broadest reasonable construction).

As an equitable doctrine, inequitable conduct hinges on basic fairness. "[T]he remedy imposed by a court of equity should be commensurate with the violation." Because inequitable conduct renders an entire patent (or even a patent family) unenforceable, as a general rule, this doctrine should only be applied in instances where the patentee's misconduct resulted in the unfair benefit of receiving an unwarranted claim. * * * After all, the patentee obtains no advantage from misconduct if the patent would have issued anyway. * * * Moreover, enforcement of an otherwise valid patent does not injure the public merely because of misconduct, lurking somewhere in patent prosecution, that was immaterial to the patent's issuance.

Although but-for materiality generally must be proved to satisfy the materiality prong of inequitable conduct, this court recognizes an exception in cases of affirmative egregious misconduct. This exception to the general rule requiring but-for proof incorporates elements of the early unclean hands cases before the Supreme Court, which dealt with "deliberately planned and carefully executed scheme[s]" to defraud the PTO and the courts. When the patentee has engaged in affirmative acts of egregious misconduct, such as the filing of an unmistakably false affidavit, the misconduct is material. * * * After all, a patentee is unlikely to go to great lengths to deceive the PTO with a falsehood unless it believes that the falsehood will affect issuance of the patent. * * * Because neither mere nondisclosure of prior art references to the PTO nor failure to mention prior art references in an affidavit constitutes affirmative egregious misconduct, claims of inequitable conduct that are based on such omissions require proof of but-for materiality. By creating an exception to punish affirmative egregious acts without penalizing the failure to disclose information that would not have changed the issuance decision, this court strikes a necessary balance between encouraging

> honesty before the PTO and preventing unfounded accusations of inequitable conduct.

Therasense, Inc. v. Becton, Dickinson & Co., 649 F.3d 1276, 1287-1293 (Fed. Cir. 2011)(en banc). While all the judges appeared to agree on the specific intent requirement, four dissenting judges argued in favor of the PTO's "Rule 56" standard for materiality, which only requires that there be a substantial likelihood that a reasonable examiner would consider the information important in deciding whether to allow the application. In your opinion, will the majority's higher "but-for" standard of materiality provide sufficient incentives for patent applicants to comply with the disclosure obligations the PTO places on them? Is the court's "affirmative egregious misconduct" exception to the "but-for" materiality standard sufficiently clear to avoid the problematic disclosure and litigation practices that had become associated with the inequitable conduct defense? In circumstances other than those involving "affirmative egregious misconduct," could a district court find a claim valid and at the same time find inequitable conduct as to the same claim? The majority clearly is concerned about the draconian results of finding inequitable conduct. Should district courts be authorized, after weighing the equities, to devise less extreme remedies?

The PTO has given notice of proposed rulemaking to adopt the Federal Circuit's "but-for" materiality standard for its Rule 56 duty to disclose. 76 Fed. Reg. No. 140, 43631 (July 21, 2011). Why might it choose to do this? Should it include a requirement that applicants assist the PTO by explaining why submitted prior art is deemed relevant?

The America Invents Act also addresses the inequitable conduct litigation problems discussed in the *Therasense* decision. AIA § 12 provides that patentees may, through a "supplemental examination," effectively insulate themselves from an inequitable conduct challenge or defense in later litigation. Under this new procedure, which resembles an *ex parte* reexamination, the patentee can submit any form of potentially relevant information that was not considered or was inadequately considered or was incorrect during prosecution. If the PTO determines that the information does not present a substantial new question of patentability, or that the patent remains valid notwithstanding the information, that information cannot later be asserted in litigation to support an inequitable conduct defense. To be effective, the supplemental examination must be requested before a challenger raises an allegation of inequitable conduct in a declaratory judgment action. The patentee must wait to file an infringement action until the supplemental examination is completed, in order to be shielded against an inequitable conduct defense in that litigation. Pub. L. No. 112-29 § 12, 125 Stat. 325 (2011) (adding a new 35 U.S.C. § 257).

Supplemental examinations will become available on September 16, 2012, and will apply in the case of all patents, whether issued before or after the effective date. If the supplemental examination reveals "material fraud," the PTO is authorized to notify the Attorney General for "such further action as the Attorney General may deem appropriate." *Id.* at § 12 .

### c. Patent Invalidity

*Page 341: Insert the following text directly after the first full paragraph:*

In Microsoft Corp. v. i4i Partnership, __ U.S. __, 131 S.Ct. 2238, 180 L.Ed.2d 131 (2011), the Supreme Court rejected challenges to the rule that patent invalidity must be proved by clear and convincing evidence, when asserted as a defense to an infringement claim. The Court found that even though the clear and convincing evidence rule is not expressly specified in Patent Act § 282, it was well established at common law that the presumption of patent validity must be overcome with clear and convincing evidence, and Congress intended to codify that common-law understanding. The Court likewise rejected arguments that a preponderance of the evidence standard should apply at least where the evidence of invalidity before the fact-finder was not before the PTO during the examination process. The Court recognized that the rationale underlying the presumption of validity—that the PTO applied its special expertise in approving the claim—is diminished in such circumstances. However, it found no precedent for a fluctuating standard of proof. And since Congress intended to adopt the common-law standard, Congress intended to apply the standard to all patent validity challenges, regardless of the nature of the challenger's proof. The Court noted, however, that a district court could properly instruct the jury that it may assign greater weight to evidence that was unavailable to the PTO, than to evidence that was.

*Page 342: Insert the following at the end of the carry-over paragraph at the top of page 342:*

In *Medimmune, supra,* the Supreme Court ruled that a patent licensee that believes that its products do not infringe the patent and accordingly are not subject to royalty payments is "not required . . . to break or terminate its . . . license agreement before seeking a declaratory judgment in federal court that the underlying patent is . . . not infringed." On May 20, 2013, the Court granted *certiorari* to consider whether, in such a declaratory judgment action, the licensee has the burden to prove that its products do not infringe the patent, or whether (as in the case in all other patent litigation, including other declaratory judgment actions), the patentee must prove infringement. See *Meditronic, Inc. v. Boston Scientific Corp.,* __ U.S. __, __ S.Ct. __, 2013 W.L. 1127900 (2013).

### d. Prior Use

*Page 343:Replace the last two paragraphs of subsection d with the following:*

The America Invents Act, § 5, substantially expands the § 273 prior user defense described above. As amended, § 273 (a) provides:

**§ 273. Defense to infringement based on prior commercial use**

(a) IN GENERAL.—A person shall be entitled to a defense under section 282(b) with respect to subject matter consisting of a process, or consisting of a machine, manufacture, or composition of matter used in a manufacturing or other commercial process, that would otherwise infringe a claimed invention being asserted against the person if—

(1) such person, acting in good faith, commercially used the subject matter in the United States, either in connection with an internal commercial use or an actual arm's length sale or other arm's length commercial transfer of a useful end result of such commercial use; and

(2) such commercial use occurred at least 1 year before the earlier of either—

(A) the effective filing date of the claimed invention; or

(B) the date on which the claimed invention was disclosed to the public in a manner that qualified for the exception from prior art under section 102(b).

35 U.S.C. § 273(a). This new prior commercial user defense applies in the case of any patent issued on or after September 16, 2011. Pub. L. No. 112-29 § 5(c), 125 Stat. 297, 299 (2011). As in the case of the pre-AIA version of the prior user defense, persons asserting this defense must establish it by clear and convincing evidence. 35 U.S.C. § 273(b). The new defense may only be asserted by the person who "performed or directed the performance of the commercial use described in subsection (a), or by an entity that controls, is controlled by, or is under common control with such person." *Id.,* § 273(e)(1)(A). The defense cannot be licensed or assigned or transferred to another person except as part of a good-faith transaction transferring the entire

enterprise or line of business to which the defense relates. *Id.,* § 273(e)(1)(B). If an effective assignment or transfer is made, the recipient of the defense may only assert it at sites where the prior commercial use was being made prior to the transfer or the patent's effective filing date, whichever is later. *Id.*, § 273(e)(1)(C). The defense is unavailable to persons who derived the subject matter of the commercial use from the patentee. *Id.,*§ 273(e)(2). Moreover, the prior commercial user defense generally cannot be asserted against university-owned patents. *Id.,* § 273(e)(5).

What might have motivated Congress to expand the prior user defense beyond the context of patented business methods? Why withhold the prior commercial user defense in the case of patents owned by Universities?

The expanded prior commercial use defense applies, under § 273(a), to a "process, or * * * a machine, manufacture, or composition of matter used in a manufacturing or other commercial process." How broad is this subject matter? What constitutes a "commercial process" or the "internal commercial use" that the defendant must have made a year prior to the effective filing date or disclosure? In the final Senate floor debate, Senator Kyl provided some insights:

> Subsection (a) expands the defense beyond just processes to also cover products that are used in a manufacturing or other commercial process. Generally, products that are sold to consumers will not need a PCU defense over the long term. As soon as the product is sold to the public, any invention that is embodied or otherwise inherent in that product becomes prior art and cannot be patented by another party, or even by the maker of the product after the grace period has expired. Some products, however, consist of tools or other devices that are used only by the inventor inside his closed factory. Others consist of substances that are exhausted in a manufacturing process and never become accessible to the public. Such products will not become prior art. Revised section 273 therefore allows the defense to be asserted with respect to such products.

> The defense can also be asserted for products that are not used to make a useful end result that is sold to others, but that are used in an internal commercial process. This would include, for example, customized software that is used to run a company's human resources system. So long as use of the product is integrated into an ongoing commercial process, and not merely fleeting or experimental or incidental to the enterprise's operations, the PCU defense can be asserted with respect of that product.

157 Cong. Rec. S5430 (daily ed. September 8, 2011) (statement of Sen. Kyle). See also 35 U.S.C. § 273(a)(c) (premarketing regulatory review and nonprofit laboratory use deemed "commercial"). After the patent issues, the prior commercial user who qualifies under § 273(a) will enjoy a defense against infringement if he continues to use the patented machine, manufacture or composition of matter in a manufacturing or other commercial process. Will he have any defense if he *makes* the patented manufacture, machine or composition of matter that he uses? What if he sells or imports it? Section 273(d) provides that "the sale or other disposition of a useful *end result* by a person entitled to assert a defense under this section in connection with a patent with respect to that useful end result shall exhaust the patent owner's rights under the patent to the extent that such rights would have been exhausted had such sale or other disposition been made by the patent owner." Why is this provision needed?

Are there any potential constitutional objections to newly amended § 273? Expansion of the prior user defense would appear to encourage inventors to retain their inventions as trade secrets, rather than apply for patents and make the associated disclosure that patent law is meant to evoke. Why might Congress have deemed it appropriate to encourage non-disclosure of inventions in this manner? In the Senate floor debate, Senator Kyl offered the following justification:

> The PCU defense is principally designed to protect the use of manufacturing processes. For many manufacturing processes, the patent system presents a Catch-22: If the manufacturer patents the process, he effectively discloses it to

> the world. But patents for processes that are used in closed factories are difficult to police. It is all but impossible to know if someone in a factory in China is infringing such a patent. As a result, unscrupulous foreign and domestic manufacturers will simply used the invention in secret without paying licensing fees. Patenting such manufacturing processes effectively amounts to giving away the invention to competitors. On the other hand, if the U.S. manufacturer does not patent the process, a subsequent party may obtain a patent for it, and the U.S. manufacturer will be forced to stop using a process that he was the first to invent and which he has been using for years.
>
> The prior-commercial-use defense provides relief to U.S. manufacturers from this Catch-22, allowing them to make long-term use of a manufacturing process without having to give it away to competitors or run the risk that it will be patented out from under them.

157 Cong. Rec., *supra,* at S5430. Is this justification persuasive?

## 2. Remedies

*Page 360, Note 1: Insert the following directly before the first paragraph, at the top of the page:*

The America Invents Act § 17 adds a new § 298 to the Patent Act, which provides:

> The failure of an infringer to obtain the advice of counsel with respect to any allegedly infringed patent, or the failure of the infringer to present such advice to the court or jury, may not be used to prove that the accused infringer willfully infringed the patent or that the infringer intended to induce infringement of the patent.

Pub. L. No. 112-29 § 17, 125 Stat. 329 (2011) (adding new 35 U.S.C. § 298). This provision became September 16, 2011.

*Page 360-62: Delete Note 2 and substitute the following:*

2. *Injunctive Relief.* What are the practical implications of a general rule that, absent exceptional circumstances, courts must issue permanent injunctions against patent infringement? Would the presence of such a rule be likely to change the behavior of parties to business transactions? Would it be likely to change the behavior of patent litigants?

In Robert Bosch LLC v. Pylon Manufacturing Corp., 659 F.3d 1142 (Fed. Cir. 2011), the Court of Appeals for the Federal Circuit clarified the impact of the *eBay* ruling on the granting of injunctions:

> Prior to the Supreme Court's decision in *eBay*, this court followed the general rule that a permanent injunction will issue once infringement and validity have been adjudged, absent a sound reason to deny such relief. In addition, at least in the context of preliminary injunctive relief, we applied an express presumption of irreparable harm upon finding that a plaintiff was likely to succeed on the merits of a patent infringement claim. * * * Based on our case law, district courts also have applied a presumption of irreparable harm following judgment of infringement and validity to support the issuance of permanent injunctions. * * * [3]
>
> In *eBay,* the Supreme Court made clear that "broad classifications" and "categorical rule[s]" have no place in this inquiry. 547 U.S. at 393. Instead, courts are to exercise their

---

[3] Indeed, applying this presumption to permanent injunctions was entirely reasonable at the time, given that "[t]he standard for a preliminary injunction is essentially the same as for a permanent injunction with the exception that the plaintiff must show a likelihood of success on the merits rather than actual success." *Amoco Prod. Co. v. Village of Gambell,* 480 U.S. 531, 546 n. 12 (1987).

discretion in accordance with traditional principles of equity. The Supreme Court, however, did not expressly address the presumption of irreparable harm, and our subsequent cases have not definitively clarified whether that presumption remains intact. * * * Our statements on this topic have led one district court judge to conclude that "the presumption of irreparable harm is at best on life support." *Red Bend Ltd. v. Google, Inc.,* 2011 WL 1288503, at *18 (D.Mass. Mar.31, 2011). We take this opportunity to put the question to rest and confirm that *eBay* jettisoned the presumption of irreparable harm as it applies to determining the appropriateness of injunctive relief. In so holding, we join at least two of our sister circuits that have reached the same conclusion as it relates to a similar presumption in copyright infringement matters. *See Perfect 10, Inc. v. Google, Inc.,* 653 F.3d 976, 981 (9th Cir.2011) ("[W]e conclude that our longstanding rule that a showing of a reasonable likelihood of success on the merits in a copyright infringement claim raises a presumption of irreparable harm is clearly irreconcilable with the reasoning of the Court's decision in *eBay* and has therefore been effectively overruled."); *Salinger v. Colting,* 607 F.3d 68, 76–78 (2d Cir.2010) (finding that *eBay* abrogated the presumption of irreparable harm in copyright cases).

Although *eBay* abolishes our general rule that an injunction normally will issue when a patent is found to have been valid and infringed, it does not swing the pendulum in the opposite direction. In other words, even though a successful patent infringement plaintiff can no longer rely on presumptions or other short-cuts to support a request for a permanent injunction, it does not follow that courts should entirely ignore the fundamental nature of patents as property rights granting the owner the right to exclude. Indeed, this right has its roots in the Constitution, as the Intellectual Property Clause of the Constitution itself refers to inventors' "*exclusive* Right to their respective ... Discoveries." U.S. Const. art. I, § 8, cl. 8 (emphasis added). Although the Supreme Court disapproved of this court's absolute reliance on the patentee's right to exclude as a basis for our prior rule favoring

> injunctions, that does not mean that the nature of patent rights has no place in the appropriate equitable analysis. *See eBay,* 547 U.S. at 392 ("According to the Court of Appeals, this statutory right to exclude alone justifies its general rule in favor of permanent injunctive relief. But the creation of a right is distinct from the provision of remedies for violations of that right."). While the patentee's right to exclude alone cannot justify an injunction, it should not be ignored either.
>
> The abolition of categorical rules and the district court's inherent discretion to fashion equitable relief, moreover, also do not mandate that district courts must act on a clean slate. "Discretion is not whim, and limiting discretion according to legal standards helps promote the basic principle of justice that like cases should be decided alike." *eBay,* 547 U.S. at 395 (Roberts, J., concurring). In this area, as others, "a page of history is worth a volume of logic" when "it comes to discerning and applying those standards." *Id.* This wisdom is particularly apt in traditional cases, such as this, where the patentee and adjudged infringer both practice the patented technology. *See id.* at 396–97 (Kennedy, J., concurring) (contrasting the relevant considerations in traditional patent infringement actions with certain cases arising now "in which firms use patents not as a basis for producing and selling goods but, instead, primarily for obtaining licensing fees," "[w]hen the patented invention is but a small component of the product," and those involving "the burgeoning number of patents over business methods").

*Id.,* at 1148-50. What kinds of evidence might a patentee rely on to make the necessary showing of irreparable harm? See *Id.* (District court should have found irreparable harm when plaintiff provided evidence of (1) the parties' direct competition; (2) loss in market share and access to potential customers resulting from defendant's introduction of infringing product; and (3) defendant's lack of financial wherewithal to satisfy a judgment.)

# II. PLANT PATENTS

*Pages 373-375: replace the materials of Note 1, beginning with the second full paragraph on page 373, with the following:*

Section 162 does not, however, directly address a related problem: What sort of "printed publication" will disqualify a plant patent for lack of novelty under 35 U.S.C. § 102? The Court of Customs and Patent Appeals addressed the "printed publication" question in *Application of* LeGrice, 301 F.2d 929 (C.C.P.A.1962). In *LeGrice*, the patent applicant's roses had been depicted and described in English publications more than a year before he filed his United States patent application. The publications included color photographs and descriptions such as the following:

> Glowing dark scarlet with dusky velvety sheen. Single blooms carried in large trusses. Size when open 3-in. in diameter. Very fragrant. Vigorous. Foliage dark green and abundant. Bedding. Trail Ground Certificate, 1945. Prune 34.

*Id.*, 301 F.2d at 931. The *LeGrice* court held that the provisions of § 102(b) were fully applicable, and that they should be interpreted in the same manner for plant patents as for utility patents. Utility patent opinions specified that the printed publication must be sufficiently full, clear and exact to enable a person skilled in the relevant art to make or practice the invention. The English publications did not enable anyone to "make" the applicant's rose. The applicant's roses were the result of cross-pollenization, but even identification of the parent plants would not be sufficiently enabling, since "the principles of heredity and plant genetics introduce such variables that no two seeds from the parent cross can be expected to produce identical plants." *Id.*, 301 F.2d at 938. Thus, the statutory bar had not been triggered.

Forty-two years later, in *In re* Elsner, 381 F.3d 1125 (Fed. Cir. 2004), the Court of Appeals for the Federal Circuit found that a description such as that in *LeGrice*, coupled with foreign sales of the described plant, could be sufficient to trigger the §102(b) statutory bar. In that case, Elsner, a German plant breeder, had applied for a

European Community Plant Variety Rights Certificate for a new type of geranium. The application was published. Elsner later withdrew the application, but sold the geranium in Europe. Likewise, Zary filed a Plant Breeder's Rights application in South Africa claiming a variety of new rose plant. That application was subsequently published, and the rose was sold in South Africa and Zambia. More than a year after these events took place, both breeders filed applications for U.S. plant patents. In finding a potential § 102(b) bar, the Federal Circuit reasoned:

> Prior art under § 102(b) must sufficiently describe a claimed invention to have placed the public in possession of that invention. The proper test of a publication as a § 102(b) bar is "whether one skilled in the art to which the invention pertains could take the description of the invention in the printed publication and combine it with his own knowledge of the particular art and from this combination be put in possession of the invention on which a patent is sought." *LeGrice,* 301 F.2d at 939. In particular, one must be able to make the claimed invention without undue experimentation.
>
> It is undisputed that the PBR applications were published more than one year prior to the effective filing dates of Appellants' respective applications and that the applications fully disclose the claimed plants. It is also clear that the foreign sales of the Pendec geranium and the JA Copper rose are not themselves § 102(b) prior art against the applications; that is, those foreign sales themselves do not constitute an on-sale bar. Ordinarily, foreign sales of an invention in combination with a publication will not constitute a bar because such a result would circumvent the established rules that neither non-enabling publications nor foreign sales can bar one's right to a patent. What sets this case apart is that it deals with plant patents* * * .
>
> * * * In the case of plant patents, the touchstone of the statutory subject matter is asexual reproduction of a unique biological organism. When a publication identifies the plant that is invented or discovered and a foreign sale occurs that

> puts one of ordinary skill in the art in possession of the plant itself, which, based on the level of ordinary skill in the art, permits asexual reproduction without undue experimentation, that combination of facts and events so directly conveys the essential knowledge of the invention that the sale combines with the publication to erect a statutory bar. In any event, the inventor is in control of the activities relating to his invention, and avoidance of a bar is accomplished by making a timely filing at the PTO.
>
> Appellants' PBR applications disclosed the claimed plant varieties, but concededly do not, by themselves, enable the skilled artisan to practice the claimed inventions or reproduce the plants. However, because the public may have had access to the claimed inventions through the foreign sales of the plants, from which the claimed plants may be reproduced, it may fairly be said that the PBR applications are adequately enabled. Because the published applications, combined with the foreign sales of the plants, placed the claimed inventions in the possession of the public, we therefore hold that they are proper § 102(b) anticipatory references that may bar patentability.

*In re Elsner*, 381 F.3d at 1128. While the Federal Circuit agreed that the prior publications, coupled with foreign sales *could* trigger the § 102(b) statutory bar, it remanded because the Board had not specifically determined whether a skilled artisan would have known of the foreign sales. How might a Court apply the new novelty and non-obviousness provisions of the America Invents Act to the same facts?

## III. DESIGN PATENTS

## A. THE LAW OF DESIGN PATENTS

*Page 396: At the end of Note 1, add the following:*

Will this issue of "experimental use" continue to exist under the America Invents Act?

*Page 400: At the end of Note 5, second paragraph, add the following:*

Congress recently enacted legislation to implement the Hague Agreement Concerning International Registration of Industrial Designs, which will permit American design owners to obtain design protection in multiple nations through a single international application procedure. By filing a single standardized application in English with the P.T.O., a U.S. design owner can apply for design protection in each country that is a party to the treaty. Foreign registration renewals and fee payments will also be simplified. See 35 U.S.C. §§ 381-90. Of course, as noted above, design protection procured in other member countries will likely take a *sui* generis form, rather than the form of a patent.

# CHAPTER FOUR

# COPYRIGHT

* * *

## III. THE EXCLUSIVE RIGHTS OF COPYRIGHT AND THEIR INFRINGEMENT

* * *

## E. THE EXCLUSIVE RIGHT TO DISTRIBUTE COPIES OR PHONORECORDS OF THE COPYRIGHTED WORK TO THE PUBLIC BY SALE OR OTHER TRANSFER OF OWNERSHIP OR BY RENTAL, LEASE, OR LENDING

* * *

### 1. The Doctrine of First Sale

*Page 550: At the top of the page, directly after the citation to the U.S. Copyright Office Report on the Droit de Suite, add the following:*

A federal district court in California has recently ruled that the California *droit de suite* statute discussed above is unconstitutional. *Estate of Graham v. Sotheby's, Inc.*, 860 F.Supp.2d 1117 (C.D.Ca. 2012). The court reasoned that the California Resale Royalties Act had "the practical effect of controlling commerce occurring wholly outside the boundaries of California," and thus violated the U.S. Constitution's Commerce Clause. *Id.,* at 1125. The court found it unnecessary to address arguments that the Act was preempted by the U.S. Copyright Act. In a footnote, the court observed that:

> "enforcement of the CRRA has been spotty. The *New York Times* recently reported that, since the CRRA was passed in 1977, approximately 400 artists have received a total of $328,000 in resale royalties. Patricia Cohen, *Artists File Lawsuits, Seeking Royalties,* N.Y. Times, Nov. 1, 2011. A 1986 survey of artists conducted by the Bay Area Lawyers for the Arts found that 32% of respondents "said dealers had refused to give them the name or address of the buyer or even the resale price, despite their right under the [CRRA] to assign collection of the royalty to another."

*Id.,* at 1121, n3 (quoting Reddy, *The Droit de Suite: Why American Fine Artists Should Have a Right to a Resale Royalty,* 15 Loy. L.A. Ent. L. Rev. 509, 523 (1995).

## 2. The Importation Right

*Pages 550-559: Replace the text in Section 2. The Importation Right, with the following:*

### Kirtsaeng v. John Wiley & Sons, Inc.

United States Supreme Court, 2013.
568 U.S. __, 133 S.Ct. 1351, 185 L.Ed.2d 392.

Justice BREYER delivered the opinion of the Court.

Section 106 of the Copyright Act grants "the owner of copyright under this title" certain "exclusive rights," including the right "to distribute copies ... of the copyrighted work to the public by sale or other transfer of ownership." 17 U.S.C. § 106(3). These rights are qualified, however, by the application of various limitations set forth in the next several sections of the Act, §§ 107 through 122. Those sections, typically entitled "Limitations on exclusive rights," include, for example, the principle of "fair use" (§ 107), permission for limited library archival reproduction, (§ 108), and the doctrine at issue here, the "first sale" doctrine (§ 109).

Section 109(a) sets forth the "first sale" doctrine as follows:

> "Notwithstanding the provisions of section 106(3) [the section that grants the owner exclusive distribution rights], the owner of a particular copy or phonorecord *lawfully made under this title* ... is entitled, without the authority of the copyright owner, to sell or otherwise dispose of the possession of that copy or phonorecord." (Emphasis added.)

Thus, even though § 106(3) forbids distribution of a copy of, say, the copyrighted novel Herzog without the copyright owner's permission, § 109(a) adds that, once a copy of Herzog has been lawfully sold (or its ownership otherwise lawfully transferred), the buyer of that *copy* and subsequent owners are free to dispose of it as they wish. In copyright jargon, the "first sale" has "exhausted" the copyright owner's § 106(3) exclusive distribution right.

What, however, if the copy of Herzog was printed abroad and then initially sold with the copyright owner's permission? Does the "first sale" doctrine still apply? Is the buyer, like the buyer of a domestically manufactured copy, free to bring the copy into the United States and dispose of it as he or she wishes?

To put the matter technically, an "importation" provision, § 602(a)(1), says that

> "[i]mportation into the United States, without the authority of the owner of copyright under this title, of copies ... of a work that have been acquired outside the United States is an infringement of the exclusive right to distribute copies ... *under section 106....*" 17 U.S.C. § 602(a)(1) (emphasis added).

Thus § 602(a)(1) makes clear that importing a copy without permission violates the owner's exclusive distribution right. But in doing so, § 602(a)(1) refers explicitly to the *§ 106(3)* exclusive distribution right. As we have just said, § 106 is by its terms "[s]ubject to" the various doctrines and principles contained in §§ 107 through 122, including § 109(a)'s "first sale" limitation. Do those same modifications apply—in particular, does the "first sale" modification apply—when considering whether § 602(a)(1) prohibits importing a copy?

In *Quality King Distributors, Inc. v. L'anza Research Int'l, Inc.*, 523 U.S. 135, 145 (1998), we held that § 602(a)(1)'s reference to § 106(3)'s exclusive distribution right incorporates the later subsections' limitations, including, in particular, the "first sale" doctrine of § 109. Thus, it might seem that, § 602(a)(1) notwithstanding, one who buys a copy abroad can freely import that copy into the United States and dispose of it, just as he could had he bought the copy in the United States.

But *Quality King* considered an instance in which the copy, though purchased abroad, was initially manufactured in the United States (and then sent abroad and sold). This case is like *Quality King* but for one important fact. The copies at issue here were manufactured abroad. That fact is important because § 109(a) says that the "first sale" doctrine applies to "a particular copy or phonorecord *lawfully made under this title*." And we must decide here whether the five words, "lawfully made under this title," make a critical legal difference.

Putting section numbers to the side, we ask whether the "first sale" doctrine applies to protect a buyer or other lawful owner of a copy (of a copyrighted work) lawfully manufactured abroad. Can that buyer bring that copy into the United States (and sell it or give it away) without obtaining permission to do so from the copyright owner? Can, for example, someone who purchases, say at a used bookstore, a book printed abroad subsequently resell it without the copyright owner's permission?

In our view, the answers to these questions are, yes. We hold that the "first sale" doctrine applies to copies of a copyrighted work lawfully made abroad.

I

A

Respondent, John Wiley & Sons, Inc., publishes academic textbooks. Wiley obtains from its authors various foreign and domestic copyright assignments, licenses and permissions—to the point that we can, for present purposes, refer to Wiley as the relevant American copyright owner. Wiley often assigns to its wholly owned foreign subsidiary, John Wiley & Sons (Asia) Pty Ltd., rights to publish, print, and sell Wiley's English language textbooks abroad. Each copy of a Wiley Asia foreign edition will likely contain language making clear that the copy is to be sold only in a particular country or geographical region outside the United States.

For example, a copy of Wiley's American edition says, "Copyright © 2008 John Wiley & Sons, Inc. All rights reserved.... Printed in the United States of America." J. Walker, Fundamentals of Physics, p. vi (8th ed. 2008). A copy of Wiley Asia's Asian edition of that book says:

> "Copyright © 2008 John Wiley & Sons (Asia) Pty Ltd[.] All rights reserved. This book is authorized for sale in Europe, Asia, Africa, and the Middle East only and may be not exported out of these territories. Exportation from or importation of this book to another region without the Publisher's authorization is illegal and is a violation of the Publisher's rights. The Publisher may take legal action to enforce its rights.... Printed in Asia." J. Walker, Fundamentals of Physics, p. vi (8th ed. 2008 Wiley Int'l Student ed.).

Both the foreign and the American copies say:

> "No part of this publication may be reproduced, stored in a retrieval system, or transmitted in any form or by any means ... except as permitted under Sections 107 or 108 of the 1976 United States Copyright Act."

The upshot is that there are two essentially equivalent versions of a Wiley textbook, each version manufactured and sold with Wiley's permission: (1) an American version printed and sold in the United States, and (2) a foreign version manufactured and sold abroad. And Wiley makes certain that copies of the second version state that they are not to be taken (without permission) into the United States.

Petitioner, Supap Kirtsaeng, a citizen of Thailand, moved to the United States in 1997 to study mathematics at Cornell University. He paid for his education with the help of a Thai Government scholarship which required him to teach in Thailand for 10 years on his return. Kirtsaeng successfully completed his undergraduate courses at Cornell, successfully completed a Ph.D. program in mathematics at the University of Southern California, and then, as promised, returned to Thailand to teach. While he was studying in the United States, Kirtsaeng asked his friends and family in Thailand to buy copies of foreign edition English-language textbooks at Thai book shops, where they sold at low prices, and mail them to him in the United States. Kirtsaeng would then sell them, reimburse his family and friends, and keep the profit.

B

In 2008 Wiley brought this federal lawsuit against Kirtsaeng for copyright infringement. Wiley claimed that Kirtsaeng's unauthorized importation of its books and his later resale of those books amounted to an infringement of Wiley's § 106(3) exclusive right to distribute as well as § 602's related import prohibition. Kirtsaeng replied that the books he had acquired were "'lawfully made' " and that he had acquired them legitimately. Thus, in his view, § 109(a)'s "first sale" doctrine permitted him to resell or otherwise dispose of the books without the copyright owner's further permission.

The District Court held that Kirtsaeng could not assert the "first sale" defense because, in its view, that doctrine does not apply to "foreign-manufactured goods" (even if made abroad with the copyright owner's permission). * * *

On appeal, a split panel of the Second Circuit agreed with the District Court. It pointed out that § 109(a)'s "first sale" doctrine applies only to "the owner of a particular copy ... *lawfully made under this title.*" And, in the majority's view, this language means that the "first sale" doctrine does not apply to copies of American copyrighted works manufactured abroad. A dissenting judge thought that the words "lawfully made under this title" do not refer "to a place of manufacture" but rather "focu[s] on whether a particular copy was manufactured lawfully under" America's copyright statute, and that "the lawfulness of the manufacture of a particular copy should be judged by U.S. copyright law."

* * *

II

We must decide whether the words "lawfully made under this title" restrict the scope of § 109(a)'s "first sale" doctrine geographically. The Second Circuit, the Ninth Circuit, Wiley, and the Solicitor General (as *amicus*) all read those words as imposing a form of *geographical* limitation. The Second Circuit held that they limit the "first sale" doctrine to particular copies "made in territories *in which the Copyright Act is law,*" which (the Circuit says) are copies "manufactured domestically," not "outside of the United States." 654 F.3d, at 221–222 (emphasis added). * * * And the Ninth Circuit has held that those words limit the "first sale" doctrine's applicability (1) to copies lawfully made in the United States, and (2) to copies lawfully made outside the United States but initially sold in the United States with the copyright owner's permission. *Denbicare U.S.A. Inc. v. Toys "R" Us, Inc.,* 84 F.3d 1143, 1149–1150 (1996).

Under any of these geographical interpretations, § 109(a)'s "first sale" doctrine would not apply to the Wiley Asia books at issue here. And, despite an American copyright owner's permission to *make* copies abroad, one who *buys* a copy of any such book or other copyrighted work—whether at a retail store, over the Internet, or at a library sale—could not resell (or otherwise dispose of) that particular copy without further permission.

Kirtsaeng, however, reads the words "lawfully made under this title" as imposing a *non*-geographical limitation. He says that they mean made "in accordance with" or "in compliance with" the Copyright Act. In that case, § 109(a)'s "first sale" doctrine would apply to copyrighted works as long as their manufacture met the requirements of American copyright law. In particular, the doctrine would apply where, as here, copies are manufactured abroad with the permission of the copyright owner. * * *

In our view, § 109(a)'s language, its context, and the common-law history of the "first sale" doctrine, taken together, favor a *non*-geographical interpretation. We also doubt that Congress would have intended to create the practical copyright-related harms with which a geographical interpretation would threaten ordinary scholarly, artistic, commercial, and consumer activities. * * *

A

The language of § 109(a) read literally favors Kirtsaeng's nongeographical interpretation, namely, that "lawfully made under this title" means made "in accordance with" or "in compliance with" the Copyright Act. The language of § 109(a) says nothing about geography. The word "under" can mean "[i]n accordance with." 18 Oxford English Dictionary 950 (2d ed.1989). See also Black's Law Dictionary 1525 (6th ed. 1990) ("according to"). And a nongeographical interpretation provides each word of the five-word phrase with a distinct purpose. The first two words of the phrase, "lawfully made," suggest an effort to distinguish those copies that were made lawfully from those that were not, and the last three words, "under this title," set forth the standard of "lawful[ness]." Thus, the nongeographical reading is simple, it promotes a traditional copyright objective (combatting piracy), and it makes word-by-word linguistic sense.

The geographical interpretation, however, bristles with linguistic difficulties. It gives the word "lawfully" little, if any, linguistic work to do. (How could a book be *un* lawfully "made under this title"?) It imports geography into a statutory provision that says nothing explicitly about it. And it is far more complex than may at first appear.

To read the clause geographically, Wiley, like the Second Circuit and the Solicitor General, must first emphasize the word "under." Indeed, Wiley reads "under this title" to mean "in conformance with the Copyright Act *where the Copyright Act is applicable*." Wiley must then take a second step, arguing that the Act "is applicable" only in the United States. * * *

One difficulty is that neither "under" nor any other word in the phrase means "where." It might mean "subject to," but as this Court has repeatedly acknowledged, the word evades a uniform, consistent meaning. * * *

A far more serious difficulty arises out of the uncertainty and complexity surrounding the second step's effort to read the necessary geographical limitation into the word "applicable" (or the equivalent). Where, precisely, is the Copyright Act "applicable"? The Act does not instantly *protect* an American copyright holder from unauthorized piracy taking place abroad. But that fact does not mean the Act is *inapplicable* to copies made abroad. As a matter of ordinary English, one can say that a statute imposing, say, a tariff upon "any rhododendron grown in Nepal" applies to *all* Nepalese rhododendrons. And, similarly, one can say that the American Copyright Act is *applicable* to *all* pirated copies, including those printed overseas. Indeed, the Act itself makes clear that (in the Solicitor General's language) foreign-printed pirated copies are "subject to" the Act. § 602(a)(2) (referring to importation of copies "the making of which either constituted an infringement of copyright, or which would have constituted an infringement of copyright if this title had been applicable") * * *.

The appropriateness of this linguistic usage is underscored by the fact that § 104 of the Act itself says that works "*subject to protection under this title* " include unpublished works "without regard to the nationality or domicile of the author," and works "first published" in any one of the nearly 180 nations that have signed a copyright treaty with the United States. §§ 104(a), (b); 101 (defining "treaty party"). Thus, ordinary English permits us to say that the Act "applies" to an Irish manuscript lying in its author's Dublin desk drawer as well as to an original recording of a ballet performance first made in Japan and now on display in a Kyoto art gallery. * * *

The Ninth Circuit's geographical interpretation produces still greater linguistic difficulty. As we said, that Circuit interprets the "first sale" doctrine to cover both (1) copies manufactured in the United States and (2) copies manufactured abroad but first sold in the United States with the American copyright owner's permission. * * *

We can understand why the Ninth Circuit may have thought it necessary to add the second part of its definition. As we shall later describe, * * * without some such qualification a copyright holder could prevent a buyer from domestically reselling or even giving away copies of a video game made in Japan, a film made in Germany, or a dress (with a design copyright) made in China, *even* if the copyright holder has granted permission for the foreign manufacture, importation, and an initial domestic sale of the copy. A publisher such as Wiley would be free to print its books abroad, allow their importation and sale within the United States, but prohibit students from later selling their used texts at a campus bookstore. We see no way, however, to reconcile this half-geographical/half-nongeographical interpretation with the language of the phrase, "lawfully made under this title." As a matter of English, it would seem that those five words either do cover copies lawfully made abroad or they do not.

In sum, we believe that geographical interpretations create more linguistic problems than they resolve. And considerations of simplicity and coherence tip the purely linguistic balance in Kirtsaeng's, nongeographical, favor.

B

Both historical and contemporary statutory context indicate that Congress, when writing the present version of § 109(a), did not have geography in mind. In respect to history, we compare § 109(a)'s present language with the language of its immediate predecessor. That predecessor said:

> "[N]othing in this Act shall be deemed to forbid, prevent, or restrict the transfer of any copy of a copyrighted work *the possession of which has been lawfully obtained.*" Copyright Act of 1909, § 41, 35 Stat. 1084 (emphasis added).

The predecessor says nothing about geography (and Wiley does not argue that it does). So we ask whether Congress, in changing its language implicitly *introduced* a geographical limitation that previously was lacking. * * *

A comparison of language indicates that it did not. The predecessor says that the "first sale" doctrine protects "the transfer of any copy *the possession of which has been lawfully obtained.*" The present version says that "*the owner* of a particular copy or phonorecord lawfully made under this title is entitled to sell or otherwise dispose of the possession of that copy or phonorecord." What does this change in language accomplish?

The language of the former version referred to those *who are not owners* of a copy, but mere possessors who "lawfully obtained" a copy. The present version covers only those who are *owners* of a "lawfully made" copy. Whom does the change leave out? Who might have lawfully *obtained* a copy of a copyrighted work but not *owned* that copy? One answer is owners of movie theaters, who during the 1970's (and before) often *leased* films from movie distributors or filmmakers. * * * Because the theater owners had "lawfully obtained" their copies, the earlier version could be read as allowing them to sell that copy, *i.e.,* it might have given them "first sale" protection. Because the theater owners were lessees, not owners, of their copies, the change in language makes clear that they (like bailees and other lessees) cannot take advantage of the "first sale" doctrine. * * *

This objective perfectly well explains the new language of the present version, including the five words here at issue. Section 109(a) now makes clear that a lessee of a copy will *not* receive "first sale" protection but one who *owns* a copy *will* receive "first sale" protection, *provided,* of course, that the copy was "*lawfully made* " and not pirated. The new language also takes into account that a copy may be "lawfully made under this title" when the copy, say of a phonorecord, comes into its owner's possession through use of a compulsory license, which "this title" provides for elsewhere, namely, in § 115. * * *

Other provisions of the present statute also support a nongeographical interpretation. For one thing, the statute phases out the "manufacturing clause," a clause that appeared in earlier statutes and had limited importation of many copies (of copyrighted works) printed outside the United States. § 601, 90 Stat. 2588 ("Prior to July 1, 1982 ... the importation into or public distribution in the United States of copies of a work consisting preponderantly of nondramatic literary material ... is prohibited unless the portions consisting of such material have been manufactured in the United States or Canada"). The phasing out of this clause sought to equalize treatment of copies manufactured in America and copies manufactured abroad.

The "equal treatment" principle, however, is difficult to square with a geographical interpretation of the "first sale" clause that would grant the holder of an American copyright (perhaps a foreign national) permanent control over the American distribution chain (sales, resales, gifts, and other distribution) in respect to copies printed abroad but not in respect to copies printed in America. And it is particularly difficult to believe that Congress would have sought this unequal treatment while saying nothing about it and while, in a related clause (the manufacturing phase-out), seeking the opposite kind of policy goal. * * *

Finally, we normally presume that the words "lawfully made under this title" carry the same meaning when they appear in different but related sections. But doing so here produces surprising consequences. Consider:

> (1) Section 109(c) says that, despite the copyright owner's exclusive right "to display" a copyrighted work (provided in § 106(5)), the owner of a particular copy "lawfully made under this title" may publicly display it without further authorization. To interpret these words geographically would mean that one who buys a copyrighted work of art, a poster, or even a bumper sticker, in Canada, in Europe, in Asia, could not display it in America without the copyright owner's further authorization.

(2) Section 109(e) specifically provides that the owner of a particular copy of a copyrighted video arcade game "lawfully made under this title" may "publicly perform or display that game in coin-operated equipment" without the authorization of the copyright owner. To interpret these words geographically means that an arcade owner could not ("without the authority of the copyright owner") perform or display arcade games (whether new or used) originally made in Japan.

(3) Section 110(1) says that a teacher, without the copyright owner's authorization, is allowed to perform or display a copyrighted work (say, an audiovisual work) "in the course of face-to-face teaching activities"—unless the teacher knowingly used "a copy that was not lawfully made under this title." To interpret these words geographically would mean that the teacher could not (without further authorization) use a copy of a film during class if the copy was lawfully made in Canada, Mexico, Europe, Africa, or Asia.

(4) In its introductory sentence, § 106 provides the Act's basic exclusive rights to an "owner of a copyright under this title." The last three words cannot support a geographic interpretation.

* * *

C

A relevant canon of statutory interpretation favors a nongeographical reading. "[W]hen a statute covers an issue previously governed by the common law," we must presume that "Congress intended to retain the substance of the common law." *Samantar v. Yousuf,* 560 U.S. 305, ——, n. 13, 130 S.Ct. 2278, 2289–2290, n. 13 (2010). * * *

The "first sale" doctrine is a common-law doctrine with an impeccable historic pedigree. In the early 17th century Lord Coke explained the common law's refusal to permit restraints on the alienation of chattels. * * *

* * * Coke emphasizes the importance of leaving buyers of goods free to compete with each other when reselling or otherwise disposing of those goods. American law too has generally thought that competition, including freedom to resell, can work to the advantage of the consumer. * * *

The "first sale" doctrine also frees courts from the administrative burden of trying to enforce restrictions upon difficult-to-trace, readily movable goods. And it avoids the selective enforcement inherent in any such effort. Thus, it is not surprising that for at least a century the "first sale" doctrine has played an important role in American copyright law. * * *

The common-law doctrine makes no geographical distinctions; nor can we find any in *Bobbs–Merrill Co. v. Straus,* 210 U.S. 339 (1908) (where this Court first applied the "first sale" doctrine) or in § 109(a)'s predecessor provision, which Congress enacted a year later. Rather, as the Solicitor General acknowledges, "a straightforward application of *Bobbs–Merrill* " would not preclude the "first sale" defense from applying to authorized copies made overseas. And we can find no language, context, purpose, or history that would rebut a "straightforward application" of that doctrine here.

* * *

D

Associations of libraries, used-book dealers, technology companies, consumer-goods retailers, and museums point to various ways in which a geographical interpretation would fail to further basic constitutional copyright objectives, in particular "promot[ing] the Progress of Science and useful Arts." U.S. Const., Art. I, § 8, cl. 8.

The American Library Association tells us that library collections contain at least 200 million books published abroad * * *; that many others were first published in the United States but printed abroad because of lower costs; and that a geographical interpretation will likely require the libraries to obtain permission (or at least create significant uncertainty) before circulating or otherwise distributing these books. * * *

How, the American Library Association asks, are the libraries to obtain permission to distribute these millions of books? How can they find, say, the copyright owner of a foreign book, perhaps written decades ago? They may not know the copyright holder's present address. * * * And, even where addresses can be found, the costs of finding them, contacting owners, and negotiating may be high indeed. Are the libraries to stop circulating or distributing or displaying the millions of books in their collections that were printed abroad?

Used-book dealers tell us that, from the time when Benjamin Franklin and Thomas Jefferson built commercial and personal libraries of foreign books, American readers have bought used books published and printed abroad. The dealers say that they have "operat[ed] ... for centuries" under the assumption that the "first sale" doctrine applies. But under a geographical interpretation a contemporary tourist who buys, say, at Shakespeare and Co. (in Paris), a dozen copies of a foreign book for American friends might find that she had violated the copyright law. The used-book dealers cannot easily predict what the foreign copyright holder may think about a reader's effort to sell a used copy of a novel. And they believe that a geographical interpretation will injure a large portion of the used-book business.

Technology companies tell us that "automobiles, microwaves, calculators, mobile phones, tablets, and personal computers" contain copyrightable software programs or packaging. Many of these items are made abroad with the American copyright holder's permission and then sold and imported (with that permission) to the United States. A geographical interpretation would prevent the resale of, say, a car, without the permission of the holder of each copyright on each piece of copyrighted automobile software. Yet there is no reason to believe that foreign auto manufacturers regularly obtain this kind of permission from their software component suppliers, and Wiley did not indicate to the contrary when asked. Without that permission a foreign car owner could not sell his or her used car.

Retailers tell us that over $2.3 trillion worth of foreign goods were imported in 2011. American retailers buy many of these goods after a first sale abroad. And, many of these items bear, carry, or contain copyrighted "packaging, logos, labels, and product inserts and instructions for [the use of] everyday packaged goods from floor cleaners and health and beauty products to breakfast cereals." The retailers add that American sales of more traditional copyrighted works, "such as books, recorded music, motion pictures, and magazines" likely amount to over $220 billion.* * * A geographical interpretation would subject many, if not all, of them to the disruptive impact of the threat of infringement suits.

Art museum directors ask us to consider their efforts to display foreign-produced works by, say, Cy Twombly, Rene Magritte, Henri Matisse, Pablo Picasso, and others. * * * A geographical interpretation, they say, would require the museums to obtain permission from the copyright owners before they could display the work—even if the copyright owner has already sold or donated the work to a foreign museum. What are the museums to do, they ask, if the artist retained the copyright, if the artist cannot be found, or if a group of heirs is arguing about who owns which copyright?

These examples, and others previously mentioned, help explain *why* Lord Coke considered the "first sale" doctrine necessary to protect "Trade and Traffi[c], and bargaining and contracting," and they help explain *why* American copyright law has long applied that doctrine.

* * *

* * * The upshot is that copyright-related consequences along with language, context, and interpretive canons argue strongly against a geographical interpretation of § 109(a).

III

* * *

* * * Wiley and the dissent claim that a nongeographical interpretation will make it difficult, perhaps impossible, for publishers (and other copyright holders) to divide foreign and domestic markets. We concede that is so. A publisher may find it more difficult to charge different prices for the same book in different geographic markets. But we do not see how these facts help Wiley, for we can find no basic principle of copyright law that suggests that publishers are especially entitled to such rights.

The Constitution describes the nature of American copyright law by providing Congress with the power to "secur[e]" to "[a]uthors" "for limited [t]imes" the "*exclusive [r]ight to their ... [w]ritings*." Art. I, § 8, cl. 8. The Founders, too, discussed the need to grant an author a limited right to exclude competition. * * * But the Constitution's language nowhere suggests that its limited exclusive right should include a right to divide markets or a concomitant right to charge different purchasers different prices for the same book, say to increase or to maximize gain. Neither, to our knowledge, did any Founder make any such suggestion. We have found no precedent suggesting a legal preference for interpretations of copyright statutes that would provide for market divisions. * * *

* * *

IV

For these reasons we conclude that the considerations supporting Kirtsaeng's nongeographical interpretation of the words "lawfully made under this title" are the more persuasive. The judgment of the Court of Appeals is reversed * * *.

### *Notes and Questions*

1. *The doctrine of first sale and parallel imports.* The issue of "parallel imports" may arise under patent and trademark law, as well as copyright law. Generally speaking, parallel imports are goods that are legitimately manufactured by or under the authority of the U.S. intellectual property owner and sold in foreign markets. Many U.S. intellectual property owners charge significantly less for their products abroad than they do in the United States. Due to this practice, or to differences in currency values, others may be able to purchase the goods abroad, ship them to the United States and profitably resell them at lower prices than the U.S. intellectual property owner charges U.S. consumers.

When U.S. intellectual property owners sell their goods abroad, or license foreign companies to manufacture and sell them abroad, they frequently negotiate contractual provisions that prohibit the foreign purchaser/licensee from bringing the goods into the United

States or transferring them to another for the purpose of doing so. If the foreign purchaser/licensee later participates in importing the goods to the U.S., the intellectual property owner will have a cause of action against it for breach of contract. In many cases, however, the goods change hands several times before landing in the hands of the parallel importers. In such instances, the parallel importers are not in privity with the U.S. intellectual property owner, and contract law may provide no redress for the importation.

Needless to say, U.S. intellectual property owners would like to use their intellectual property rights to prohibit the parallel imports. We have considered their ability to do this under patent law (see *supra,* at pp. 297-300), and will later consider their ability to rely on trademark law to exclude the goods (see *infra,* pp. 920-33). As a general matter, what are the public policy implications of permitting or prohibiting parallel imports? What is the purpose of the first sale doctrine? Is construction of the doctrine of first sale to permit parallel imports consistent with that purpose? In the long term, will the availability of parallel imports enhance or depress competition in U.S markets? In global markets?

In her dissent, Justice Ginsburg discussed the international status of parallel imports, and the stance the United States Executive Branch has taken in international treaty negotiations:

> This case bears on the highly contentious trade issue of interterritorial exhaustion. The issue arises because intellectual property law is territorial in nature, which means that creators of intellectual property "may hold a set of parallel" intellectual property rights under the laws of different nations. There is no international consensus on whether the sale in one country of a good incorporating protected intellectual property exhausts the intellectual property owner's right to control the distribution of that good elsewhere. Indeed, the members of the World Trade Organization, "agreeing to disagree," provided in Article 6 of the Agreement on Trade–Related Aspects of Intellectual Property Rights (TRIPS), Apr. 15, 1994, 33 I.L.M. 1197, 1200, that "nothing in this Agreement shall be used to address the

issue of ... exhaustion." Similar language appears in other treaties to which the United States is a party. * * *

In the absence of agreement at the international level, each country has been left to choose for itself the exhaustion framework it will follow. One option is a national-exhaustion regime, under which a copyright owner's right to control distribution of a particular copy is exhausted only within the country in which the copy is sold. Another option is a rule of international exhaustion, under which the authorized distribution of a particular copy anywhere in the world exhausts the copyright owner's distribution right everywhere with respect to that copy. The European Union has adopted the intermediate approach of regional exhaustion, under which the sale of a copy anywhere within the European Economic Area exhausts the copyright owner's distribution right throughout that region. Section 602(a)(1), in my view, ties the United States to a national-exhaustion framework. The Court's decision, in contrast, places the United States solidly in the international-exhaustion camp.

* * * International exhaustion subjects copyright-protected goods to competition from lower priced imports and, to that extent, benefits consumers. Correspondingly, copyright owners profit from a national-exhaustion regime, which also enlarges the monetary incentive to create new copyrightable works. * * *

Weighing the competing policy concerns, our Government reached the conclusion that widespread adoption of the international-exhaustion framework would be inconsistent with the long-term economic interests of the United States. Accordingly, the United States has steadfastly "taken the position in international trade negotiations that domestic copyright owners should ... have the right to prevent the unauthorized importation of copies of their work sold abroad." The United States has "advanced this position in multilateral trade negotiations," including the negotiations on the TRIPS Agreement. It has also taken a dim view of our trading partners' adoption of legislation incorporating elements of international exhaustion. * * *

> Even if the text and history of the Copyright Act were ambiguous on the answer to the question this case presents—which they are not—I would resist a holding out of accord with the firm position the United States has taken on exhaustion in international negotiations. * * *

*Kirtsaeng, supra,* 133 S.Ct. at 1383-85 (Ginsburg, J., dissenting)(quoting government *amicus curiae* brief in *Quality King Distributors, Inc. v. L'Anza Research International, Inc.,* 523 U.S. 135 (1998)). Should the Executive Branch's decision to promote national exhaustion in treaty negotiations affect the Supreme Court's decision in *Kirtsaeng*?

Do U.S. copyright owners need control over parallel imports as an economic incentive to create? If the *Kirtsaeng* Court had accepted Wiley's "geographic restriction" argument and affirmed the Second Circuit's decision (holding that while goods manufactured in the U.S. and sold abroad are subject to the doctrine of first sale, goods manufactured lawfully abroad are not) what impact might that have had on the U.S. job market? As the *Kirtsaeng* Court notes, copyright owners have long argued that they need to prevent parallel imports in order successfully to divide markets—for example, to sell their goods for a higher price in affluent nations than in non-affluent nations, without the risk of arbitrage. What are the implications of enabling copyright owners to divide markets? Are the implications strictly economic in nature?

What, if any, implications does the *Kirtsaeng* decision have for parallel imports of patented goods?

In light of the *Kirtsaeng* decision, when will manufacture of copyrighted goods be "in accordance with" the United States Copyright Act? When will importation of copyrighted goods infringe under Copyright Act § 602? What does § 602, as construed in *Kirtsaeng*, give to U.S. copyright owners that they would not otherwise have under other provisions of the Copyright Act? Note § 602(a)(3)'s exceptions to § 602(a)(1)'s importation prohibition. Is the *Kirtsaeng* construction of § 602(a)(1) consistent with the existence of the exceptions?

# V. DIGITAL RIGHTS MANAGEMENT

*Page 640, Note 1, paragraph 2: Please add the following text to the end of the citation of the MGE UPS Systems case, at the bottom of the page*

(The Court of Appeals for the Fifth Circuit has subsequently withdrawn the opinion in MGE UPS Systems, Inc. v. GE Consumer and Industrial, Inc., 612 F.3d 760 ($5^{th}$ Cir. 2010), and replaced it with an opinion that takes no position on the necessity of a link between circumvention and infringement. MGE UPS Systems, Inc. v. GE Consumer and Industrial, Inc., 622 F.3d 361 ($5^{th}$ Cir. 2010)(finding instead that the defendants had not engaged in the act of circumvention)). In MDY Industries, LLC v. Blizzard Entertainment, Inc., 629 F.3d 928 ($9^{th}$ Cir. 2010), the Court of Appeals for the Ninth Circuit considered and expressly rejected the *Chamberlain* Court's construction of the DMCA: "[W]e conclude that a fair reading of the statute (supported by legislative history) indicates that Congress created a distinct anti-circumvention right under § 1201(a) without an infringement nexus requirement. Thus, even accepting the validity of the concerns expressed in *Chamberlain,* those concerns do not authorize us to override congressional intent and add a non-textual element to the statute." *Id.* at 952.

# VII. COPYRIGHT FORMALITIES: NOTICE, REGISTRATION AND DEPOSIT

## A. NOTICE OF COPYRIGHT

*Page 670, end of first full paragraph, replace citation to Golan v. Gonzales with the following:*

The Supreme Court recently upheld the constitutionality of the foreign copyright restoration provisions against challenges that the provisions exceeded Congress' authority under the Patents and Copyrights Clause and violated the First Amendment. Golan v. Holder, __U.S. __, 132 S.Ct. 873, 181 L.Ed.2d 835 (2011). In doing so, the Court relied heavily on its earlier reasoning in Eldred v. Ashcroft, 537 U.S. 186 (2003), which the case book reproduces in part at page 676.

# CHAPTER FIVE

# TRADEMARKS AND OTHER INDICATONS OF ORIGIN

* * *

## VII. RIGHTS IN INDICATIONS OF ORIGIN

## A. DIRECT INFRINGEMENT

* * *

### 3. Trademark Use and Likelihood of Confusion in the Internet Context

*Page 906-907: Insert the following decision directly before the Notes and Questions*

### Network Automation, Inc. v. Advanced Systems Concepts, Inc.

United States Court of Appeals for the Ninth Circuit, 2011.
638 F.3d 1137.

Wardlaw, Circuit Judge:

"We must be acutely aware of excessive rigidity when applying the law in the Internet context; emerging technologies require a flexible approach." Brookfield Commc'ns, Inc. v. West Coast Entm't Corp., 174 F.3d 1036, 1054 (9th Cir.1999).

Network Automation ("Network") and Advanced Systems Concepts ("Systems") are both in the business of selling job scheduling and management software, and both advertise on the Internet. Network sells its software under the mark AutoMate, while Systems' product is sold under the registered trademark ActiveBatch. Network decided to advertise its product by purchasing certain keywords, such as "ActiveBatch," which when keyed into various search engines, most prominently Google and Microsoft Bing, produce a results page showing "www. Network Automation.com" as a sponsored link. Systems' objection to Network's use of its trademark to interest viewers in Network's website gave rise to this trademark infringement action.

The district court was confronted with the question whether Network's use of ActiveBatch to advertise its products was a clever and legitimate use of readily available technology, such as Google's AdWords, or a likely violation of the Lanham Act, 15 U.S.C. § 1114. The court found a likelihood of initial interest confusion by applying the eight factors we established more than three decades ago in AMF Inc. v. Sleekcraft Boats, 599 F.2d 341 (9th Cir.1979), and reasoning that the three most important factors in "cases involving the Internet" are (1) the similarity of the marks; (2) the relatedness of the goods; and (3) the marketing channel used. The court therefore issued a preliminary injunction against Network's use of the mark ActiveBatch.

Mindful that the sine qua non of trademark infringement is consumer confusion, and that the Sleekcraft factors are but a nonexhaustive list of factors relevant to determining the likelihood of consumer confusion, we conclude that Systems' showing of a likelihood of confusion was insufficient to support injunctive relief. Therefore, we vacate the injunction and reverse and remand.

* * *

III. Discussion

"A plaintiff seeking a preliminary injunction must establish that he is likely to succeed on the merits, that he is likely to suffer irreparable harm in the absence of preliminary relief, that the balance of equities tips in his favor, and that an injunction is in the public interest." Network argues that the district court erred by ruling that Systems was likely to succeed on the merits of its trademark claim * * *.

* * *

* * *We note that the district court correctly found the prerequisite "use in commerce" in Network's use of the mark to purchase keywords to advertise its products for sale on the Internet. Previously we have assumed, without expressly deciding, that the use of a trademark as a search engine keyword that triggers the display of a competitor's advertisement is a "use in commerce" under the Lanham Act. See Playboy Enters., Inc. v. Netscape Commc'ns Corp., 354 F.3d 1020, 1024 (9th Cir.2004) We now agree with the Second Circuit that such use is a "use in commerce" under the Lanham Act. See Rescuecom Corp. v. Google Inc., 562 F.3d 123, 127 (2d Cir.2009) * * *.

This case, therefore, turns on whether Network's use of Systems' trademark is likely to cause consumer confusion. Network argues that its use of Systems' mark is legitimate "comparative, contextual advertising" which presents sophisticated consumers with clear choices. Systems characterizes Network's behavior differently, accusing it of misleading consumers by hijacking their attention with intentionally unclear advertisements. To resolve this dispute we must apply the Sleekcraft test in a flexible manner, keeping in mind that the eight factors it recited are not exhaustive, and that only some of them are relevant to determining whether confusion is likely in the case at hand.

A.

In Sleekcraft, * * * [w]e identified eight "relevant" factors for determining whether consumers would likely be confused by related goods: "[1] strength of the mark; [2] proximity of the goods; [3] similarity of the marks; [4] evidence of actual confusion; [5] marketing channels used; [6] type of goods and the degree of care likely to be exercised by the purchaser; [7] defendant's intent in selecting the mark; and [8] likelihood of expansion of the product lines." We also noted that "the list is not exhaustive," and that "[o]ther variables may come into play depending on the particular facts presented."

The Sleekcraft factors are intended as an adaptable proxy for consumer confusion, not a rote checklist. * * *

When we first confronted issues of trademark infringement and consumer confusion in the Internet context over a decade ago in Brookfield, we noted that "[w]e must be acutely aware of excessive rigidity when applying the law in the Internet context; emerging technologies require a flexible approach." There, Brookfield, a software company, marketed an entertainment database program under the mark MovieBuff. It sold the software, and offered access to the database, on its website, moviebuffonline.com. West Coast, a video retailer, had registered the mark The Movie Buff's Movie Store. West Coast operated a website using the domain name moviebuff.com, which included a film database that competed with Brookfield's product.

We held that Brookfield was likely to succeed in its claim to be the senior user of MovieBuff, and that there was a likelihood of source confusion stemming from West Coast's use of the mark in its domain name. "Heeding our repeated warnings against simply launching into a mechanical application of the eight-factor Sleekcraft test," we determined that three of the eight factors were the most important in analyzing source confusion in the context of Internet domain names: (1) the similarity of the marks; (2) the relatedness of the goods and services offered; and (3) the simultaneous use of the Internet as a marketing channel. Reasoning that the two marks were virtually identical in terms of sight, sound and meaning, that West Coast and Brookfield both offered products and services relating to movies, and that they both used the Web as a marketing and advertising device, we concluded that consumer confusion was likely, particularly given the nature of the consumers at issue, who included casual movie watchers unlikely to realize that they had mistakenly clicked on to West Coast's site when they had intended to reach Brookfield's.

Brookfield also asserted that West Coast infringed its mark by causing initial interest confusion because it had included MovieBuff in its "metatags," code not visible to web users embedded in a website to attract search engines seeking a corresponding keyword. Although were we to apply the same analysis in the metatags context as we did in the domain name context, we would easily reach the same conclusion as to each of the factors (with the possible exception of purchaser care), we declined to do so, reasoning that the "question in the metatags context is quite different." In the metatags context, the question was whether West Coast could use the mark MovieBuff in the metatags of its website to attract search engines to locate its site when the keyword "MovieBuff" was entered, a question analogous to the issue presented here. As in the domain name context, the degree of care and sophistication of the consumer was a key factor, although the outcome differed. We did not find a likelihood of source confusion because the results list from a search for "MovieBuff" would result in a list that included both Brookfield's and West Coast's websites, and if the consumer clicked on West Coast's site its own name was "prominently display[ed]." Thus a consumer was much less likely to be confused about which site he was viewing.

Finding no source confusion, we nonetheless concluded that West Coast's use of MovieBuff in its metatags was likely to cause initial interest confusion. That is, by using Brookfield's mark MovieBuff to direct persons searching for Brookfield's product to the West Coast site, West Coast derived an improper benefit from the goodwill Brookfield developed in its mark.

Five years later in Playboy, we considered the practice of "keying"—another situation analogous to that here. Netscape operated a search engine that offered an early version of a keyword advertising program. It sold lists of terms to sponsors, and when users searched for the keywords on the list, the sponsor's advertisement would be displayed on the results page. Netscape required its advertisers from the adult entertainment industry to link their ads to one such list that contained more than 400 terms, including trademarks held by Playboy. Playboy sued, contending that this practice infringed its trademarks in violation of the Lanham Act. The district court entered summary judgment in favor of Netscape.

We reversed, holding that summary judgment was inappropriate because genuine issues of material fact existed as to whether Netscape's keying practices constituted actionable infringement. Following Brookfield, we analyzed the keying issue in terms of initial interest confusion, "find[ing] insufficient evidence to defeat summary judgment on any other theory." Playboy claimed that

Netscape "misappropriated the goodwill of [its] marks by leading Internet users to competitors' websites just as West Coast ... misappropriated the goodwill of Brookfield's mark." In framing the initial interest confusion inquiry, we stressed that Playboy's infringement claim relied on the fact that the linked banner advertisements were "unlabeled," and were, therefore, more likely to mislead consumers into believing they had followed a link to Playboy's own website.

In Playboy, as in Brookfield, we applied the Sleekcraft test flexibly, determining that evidence of actual confusion was the most important factor. Playboy had introduced an expert study showing that a "statistically significant number" of Internet users searching for the terms "playboy" and "playmate" would think that Playboy itself sponsored the banner advertisements which appeared on the search results page. We noted that this study "alone probably suffices to reverse the grant of summary judgment," but we nonetheless analyzed other relevant Sleekcraft factors. As to the strength of the mark, we credited Playboy's expert reports showing it had created strong secondary meanings for "playboy" and "playmate." This suggested that consumers who entered these terms were likely searching for Playboy's products in particular. Analyzing the nature of the goods and consumer, we "presume[d] that the average searcher seeking adult-oriented materials on the Internet is easily diverted from a specific product he or she is seeking if other options, particularly graphic ones, appear more quickly." We concluded that there were genuine issues of material fact with respect to whether consumers were likely to be confused by Netscape's keying practices.

Concurring, Judge Berzon was struck by how analytically similar the keyed advertisements in Playboy were to the infringing metatags in Brookfield. We agree, and also find similarity to the use of the keyword "ActiveBatch" in this case. Judge Berzon cautioned that a broad reading of Brookfield 's metatags holding could result in a finding of initial interest confusion "when a consumer is never confused as to source or affiliation, but instead knows, or should know, from the outset that a product or web link is not related to that of the trademark holder because the list produced by the search engine so informs him." She clarified that the Playboy panel's holding was limited to "situations in which the banner advertisements are not labeled or identified."

Judge Berzon analogized the experience of browsing clearly labeled keyword advertisements to shopping at Macy's, explaining that if a shopper en route to the Calvin Klein section is diverted by a prominently displayed Charter Club (Macy's own brand) collection and never reaches the Calvin Klein collection, it could not be said that Macy's had infringed on Calvin Klein's trademark by diverting the customer to it with a clearly labeled, but more prominent display. Therefore, it would be wrong to expand the initial interest confusion theory of infringement beyond the realm of the misleading and deceptive to the context of legitimate comparative and contextual advertising.

B.

Here we consider whether the use of another's trademark as a search engine keyword to trigger one's own product advertisement violates the Lanham Act. We begin by examining the Sleekcraft factors that are most relevant to the determination whether the use is likely to cause initial interest confusion. While the district court analyzed each of the Sleekcraft factors, it identified the three most important factors as (1) the similarity of the marks, (2) the relatedness of the goods or services, and (3) the simultaneous use of the Web as a marketing channel, for any case addressing trademark infringement on the Internet. * * *

However, we did not intend Brookfield to be read so expansively as to forever enshrine these three factors—now often referred to as the "Internet trinity" or "Internet troika"—as the test for trademark infringement on the Internet. Brookfield was the first to present a claim of initial interest confusion on the Internet; we recognized at the time it would not be the last, and so emphasized flexibility over rigidity. Depending on the facts of each specific case arising on the Internet, other factors may emerge as more illuminating on the question of consumer confusion. In Brookfield, we used the "troika" factors to analyze the risk of source confusion generated by similar domain names, but we did not wholesale adopt them in the metatag analysis. * * *

Given the multifaceted nature of the Internet and the ever-expanding ways in which we all use the technology, however, it makes no sense to prioritize the same three factors for every type of potential online commercial activity. The "troika" is a particularly poor fit for the question presented here. * * * The potential infringement in this context arises from the risk that while using Systems' mark to search for information about its product, a consumer might be confused by a results page that shows a competitor's advertisement on the same screen, when that advertisement does not clearly identify the source or its product.

In determining the proper inquiry for this particular trademark infringement claim, we adhere to two long stated principles: the Sleekcraft factors (1) are non-exhaustive, and (2) should be applied flexibly, particularly in the context of Internet commerce. Finally, because the sine qua non of trademark infringement is consumer confusion, when we examine initial interest confusion, the owner of the mark must demonstrate likely confusion, not mere diversion.

We turn to an examination of each Sleekcraft factor to analyze whether there is a likelihood of consumer confusion in this case, assigning each factor appropriate weight in accordance with its relevance to the factual circumstances presented here.

1. Strength of the Mark

"The stronger a mark—meaning the more likely it is to be remembered and associated in the public mind with the mark's owner—the greater the protection it is accorded by the trademark laws." Two relevant measurements are conceptual strength and commercial strength. Conceptual strength involves classification of a mark "along a spectrum of generally increasing inherent distinctiveness as generic, descriptive, suggestive, arbitrary, or fanciful." "A mark's conceptual strength depends largely on the obviousness of its connection to the good or service to which it refers." Federal trademark "[r]egistration alone may be sufficient in an appropriate case to satisfy a determination of distinctiveness." However, "while the registration adds something on the scales, we must come to grips with an assessment of the mark itself."

Commercial strength is based on "actual marketplace recognition," and thus "advertising expenditures can transform a suggestive mark into a strong mark."

This factor is probative of confusion here because a consumer searching for a generic term is more likely to be searching for a product category. * * * That consumer is more likely to expect to encounter links and advertisements from a variety of sources. By contrast, a user searching for a distinctive term is more likely to be looking for a particular product, and therefore could be more susceptible to confusion when sponsored links appear that advertise a similar product from a different source. * * * On the other hand, if the ordinary consumers of this particular product are particularly sophisticated and knowledgeable, they might also be aware that Systems is the source of ActiveBatch software and not be confused at all.

The district court acknowledged that the parties failed to address the strength of the mark, but it concluded that the factor favors Systems. It reasoned that ActiveBatch is a suggestive mark because it "requires a mental leap from the mark to the product," and as a registered trademark it is "inherently distinctive." We agree. Because the mark is both Systems' product name and a suggestive federally registered trademark, consumers searching for the term are presumably looking for its specific product, and not a category of goods. Nonetheless, that may not be the end of the inquiry about this factor, as the sophistication of the consumers of the product may also play a role. The district court properly declined to consider commercial strength, which, as an evidence-intensive inquiry, is unnecessary at the preliminary injunction stage.

2. Proximity of the Goods

"Related goods are generally more likely than unrelated goods to confuse the public as to the producers of the goods." "[T]he danger presented is that the public will mistakenly assume there is an association between the producers of the related goods, though no such association exists." The proximity of goods is measured by whether the products are: (1) complementary; (2) sold to the same class of purchasers; and (3) similar in use and function.

The proximity of the goods was relevant in Playboy, where unsophisticated consumers were confronted with unlabeled banner advertisements that touted adult-oriented material very similar to Playboy's own products. There, we concluded that under the circumstances, the relatedness of the goods bolstered the likelihood of confusion, and therefore favored Playboy. However, the proximity of the goods would become less important if advertisements are clearly labeled or consumers exercise a high degree of care, because rather than being misled, the consumer would merely be confronted with choices among similar products. * * *

Because the products at issue here are virtually interchangeable, this factor may be helpful, but it must be considered in conjunction with the labeling and appearance of the advertisements and the degree of care exercised by the consumers of the ActiveBatch software. By weighing this factor in isolation and failing to consider whether the parties' status as direct competitors would actually lead to a likelihood of confusion, the district court allowed this factor to weigh too heavily in the analysis.

3. Similarity of the Marks

"[T]he more similar the marks in terms of appearance, sound, and meaning, the greater the likelihood of confusion." "Where the two marks are entirely dissimilar, there is no likelihood of confusion." "Similarity of the marks is tested on three levels: sight, sound, and meaning. Each must be considered as they are encountered in the marketplace."

In Sleekcraft, we concluded that the marks "Sleekcraft" and "Slickcraft" were similar in terms of sight, sound, and meaning by examining the actual situations in which consumers were likely to read, hear, and consider the meaning of the terms. Such an inquiry is impossible here where the consumer does not confront two distinct trademarks. Rather, after entering one company's mark as a search term, the consumer sees a competitor's sponsored link that displays neither company's trademarks. The district court erroneously treated "ActiveBatch," the keyword purchased by Network, as conceptually separate from ActiveBatch the trademark owned by Systems. This is an artificial distinction that does not reflect what consumers "encountered in the marketplace." Again, however, because the consumer keys in Systems' trademark, which results in Network's sponsored link, depending on the labeling and appearance of the advertisement, including whether it identifies Network's own mark, and the degree of care and sophistication of the consumer, it could be helpful in determining initial interest confusion.

4. Evidence of Actual Confusion

"[A] showing of actual confusion among significant numbers of consumers provides strong support for the likelihood of confusion." * * * However, "actual confusion is not necessary to a finding of likelihood of confusion under the Lanham Act." Indeed, "[p]roving actual confusion is difficult ... and the courts have often discounted such evidence because it was unclear or insubstantial."

In Playboy, the expert report showing a significant number of users were confused by the keying practice at issue was strong evidence that Playboy's infringement claim should be allowed to proceed. Playboy, however, was decided at the summary judgment stage, whereas here we examine a sparse record supporting preliminary injunctive relief. As the district court noted, neither Network nor Systems provided evidence regarding actual confusion, which is not surprising given the procedural posture. Therefore, while this is a relevant factor for determining the likelihood of confusion in keyword advertising cases, its importance is diminished at the preliminary injunction stage of the proceedings. The district court correctly concluded that this factor should be accorded no weight.

5. Marketing Channels

"Convergent marketing channels increase the likelihood of confusion." In Sleekcraft, the two products were sold in niche marketplaces, including boat shows, specialty retail outlets, and trade magazines. However, this factor becomes less important when the marketing channel is less obscure. Today, it would be the rare commercial retailer that did not advertise online, and the shared use of a ubiquitous marketing channel does not shed much light on the likelihood of consumer confusion. * * *

Therefore, the district court's determination that because both parties advertise on the Internet this factor weighed in favor of Systems was incorrect.

6. Type of Goods and Degree of Care

"Low consumer care ... increases the likelihood of confusion." "In assessing the likelihood of confusion to the public, the standard used by the courts is the typical buyer exercising ordinary caution.... When the buyer has expertise in the field, a higher standard is proper though it will not preclude a finding that confusion is likely. Similarly, when the goods are expensive, the buyer can be expected to exercise greater care in his purchases; again, though, confusion may still be likely."

The nature of the goods and the type of consumer is highly relevant to determining the likelihood of confusion in the keyword advertising context. A sophisticated consumer of business software exercising a high degree of care is more likely to understand the mechanics of Internet search engines and the nature of sponsored links, whereas an un-savvy consumer exercising less care is more likely to be confused. The district court determined that this factor weighed in Systems' favor because "there is generally a low degree of care exercised by Internet consumers." However, the degree of care analysis cannot begin and end at the marketing channel. We still must consider the nature and cost of the goods, and whether "the products being sold are marketed primarily to expert buyers."

In Brookfield, the websites were visited by both sophisticated entertainment industry professionals and amateur film fans, which supported the conclusion that at least some of the consumers were likely to exercise a low degree of care. In Playboy, the relevant consumer was looking for cheap, interchangeable adult-oriented material, which similarly led to our court's finding that the consumers at issue would exercise a low degree of care. In both cases, we looked beyond the medium itself and to the nature of the particular goods and the relevant consumers.

We have recently acknowledged that the default degree of consumer care is becoming more heightened as the novelty of the

Internet evaporates and online commerce becomes commonplace. In Toyota Motor Sales v. Tabari, 610 F.3d 1171 (9th Cir.2010), we vacated a preliminary injunction that prohibited a pair of automobile brokers from using Toyota's "Lexus" mark in their domain names. We determined that it was unlikely that a reasonably prudent consumer would be confused into believing that a domain name that included a product name would necessarily have a formal affiliation with the maker of the product, as "[c]onsumers who use the internet for shopping are generally quite sophisticated about such matters." The Tabari panel reasoned,

> [I]n the age of FIOS, cable modems, DSL and T1 lines, reasonable, prudent and experienced internet consumers are accustomed to such exploration by trial and error. They skip from site to site, ready to hit the back button whenever they're not satisfied with a site's contents. They fully expect to find some sites that aren't what they imagine based on a glance at the domain name or search engine summary. Outside the special case of ... domains that actively claim affiliation with the trademark holder, consumers don't form any firm expectations about the sponsorship of a website until they've seen the landing page—if then.

Id. at 1179. We further explained that we expect consumers searching for expensive products online to be even more sophisticated.* * *

Therefore the district court improperly concluded that this factor weighed in Systems' favor based on a conclusion reached by our court more than a decade ago in Brookfield * * * that Internet users on the whole exercise a low degree of care. While the statement may have been accurate then, we suspect that there are many contexts in which it no longer holds true.

7. Defendant's Intent

"When the alleged infringer knowingly adopts a mark similar to another's, reviewing courts presume that the defendant can accomplish his purpose: that is, that the public will be deceived." Nevertheless, we have also "recognized that liability for infringement may not be imposed for using a registered trademark in connection with truthful comparative advertising."

Therefore, much like the proximity of the goods, the defendant's intent may be relevant here, but only insofar as it bolsters a finding that the use of the trademark serves to mislead consumers rather than truthfully inform them of their choice of products. The district court incorrectly considered the intent factor in isolation, and concluded that it weighed in Systems' favor without first determining that Network intended to deceive consumers rather than compare its product to ActiveBatch.

8. Likelihood of Expansion of the Product Lines

"Inasmuch as a trademark owner is afforded greater protection against competing goods, a 'strong possibility' that either party may expand his business to compete with the other will weigh in favor of finding that the present use is infringing. When goods are closely related, any expansion is likely to result in direct competition." Where two companies are direct competitors, this factor is unimportant. Therefore, the district court correctly declined to consider the likelihood of expansion.

9. Other Relevant Factors

The eight Sleekcraft factors are "not exhaustive. Other variables may come into play depending on the particular facts presented." In the keyword advertising context the "likelihood of confusion will ultimately turn on what the consumer saw on the screen and reasonably believed, given the context." In Playboy, we found it important that the consumers saw banner advertisements that were "confusingly labeled or not labeled at all." We noted that clear labeling "might eliminate the likelihood of initial interest confusion that exists in this case."

The appearance of the advertisements and their surrounding context on the user's screen are similarly important here. The district court correctly examined the text of Network's sponsored links, concluding that the advertisements did not clearly identify their source. However, the district court did not consider the surrounding context. In Playboy, we also found it important that Netscape's search engine did not clearly segregate the sponsored advertisements from the objective results. Here, even if Network has not clearly identified itself in the text of its ads, Google and Bing have partitioned their search results pages so that the advertisements appear in separately labeled sections for "sponsored" links. The labeling and appearance of the advertisements as they appear on the results page includes more than the text of the advertisement, and must be considered as a whole.

C.

Given the nature of the alleged infringement here, the most relevant factors to the analysis of the likelihood of confusion are: (1) the strength of the mark; (2) the evidence of actual confusion; (3) the type of goods and degree of care likely to be exercised by the purchaser; and (4) the labeling and appearance of the advertisements and the surrounding context on the screen displaying the results page.

The district court did not weigh the Sleekcraft factors flexibly to match the specific facts of this case. It relied on the Internet "troika," which is highly illuminating in the context of domain names, but which fails to discern whether there is a likelihood of confusion in a keywords case. Because the linchpin of trademark infringement is consumer confusion, the district court abused its discretion in issuing the injunction. * * * We need not reach the three remaining preliminary injunction elements, or consider the remaining issues on appeal.

* * *

*Page 908: Add the following to the end of the Notes and Questions section:*

2. *Likelihood of confusion.* In your opinion, did the court in *Network Automation* reach the correct result? Was its reasoning persuasive? Should initial interest confusion even be deemed actionable in the sponsored link context? Is the initial interest confusion significant enough to warrant judicial relief? Is there a danger that courts will continue to penalize mere diversion of consumers?

The *Network Automation* court says that the *Sleekcraft* factors are non-exhaustive—did that court create any new factors for consideration in sponsored link settings? If so, how would you describe it/them? How heavily should it/they be weighed in relation to the other likelihood of confusion factors?

# CHAPTER SIX

# UNFAIR COMPETITION

* * *

## II. FALSE ADVERTISING

*Page 1025: Add the following to the end of the last full paragraph:*

Given ongoing questions about the proper standard for standing in § 43(a) false advertising claims, the United States Supreme Court has granted *certiorari* to consider the following question: Whether the appropriate analytic framework for determining a party's standing to maintain an action for false advertising under the Lanham Act is:

> (1) The factors set forth in *Associated Gen. Contractors of Cal, Inc. v. Cal State Council of Carpenters*, 45 U.S. 519, 537-45 (1983), as adopted by the Third, Fifth, Eighth, and Eleventh Circuits [the *Associated General Contractors* factors are: (a) the causal connection between the antitrust violation and harm to the plaintiff and whether that harm was intended to be caused; (b) the nature of the plaintiff's alleged injury, including the status of the plaintiff as consumer or competitor in the relevant market; (c) the directness or indirectness of the injury, and the related inquiry of whether the damages are speculative; (d) the potential for duplicative recovery or complex apportionment of damages; and (e) the existence of more direct victims of the alleged antitrust violation];
>
> (2) The categorical test, permitting suits only by an actual competitor, employed by the Seventh, Ninth, and Tenth Circuits; or
>
> (3) A version of the more expansive "reasonable interest" test, either as applied by the Sixth Circuit [in the case below] or as applied by the Second Circuit in prior cases.

*Static Control Components, Inc. v. Lexmark Int'l, Inc.*, __U.S. __, __ S.Ct. __, 2013 W.L. 182751 (2013). In *Static Control,*, the Court of Appeals for the Sixth Circuit held that the plaintiff alleged a cognizable interest to its business reputation and sales to remanufacturers, and sufficiently alleged that those interests were harmed, when the defendant had stated to the remanufacturers that the plaintiff was engaging in illegal conduct.